A MAT STYLE

MATTHEW CLARK

ON WRITING AND TECHNIQUE

OXFORD

UNIVERSITY PRESS

OXFORD
UNIVERSITY PRESS

8 Sampson Mews, Suite 204, Don Mills, Ontario M3C 0H5

www.oupcanada.com

Oxford University Press is a department of the University of Oxford. It furthers the University's objective of excellence in research, scholarship, and education by publishing worldwide in

Oxford New York

Auckland Cape Town Dar es Salaam Hong Kong Karachi
Kuala Lumpur Madrid Melbourne Mexico City Nairobi
New Delhi Shanghai Taipei Toronto

Oxford is a trade mark of Oxford University Press in the UK and in certain other countries

Published in Canada by Oxford University Press

Since this page cannot accommodate all the copyright notices, pages 163–7 constitute an extension of the copyright page.

National Library of Canada Cataloguing in Publication Data

Clark, Matthew, 1948–
     A matter of style : on writing and technique

Includes bibliographical references and index.
ISBN-10: 0-19-541762-3   ISBN-13: 978-0-19-541762-3

1. English language—Style. I. Title.

PE1421.C56 2002   808'.042   C2002-900635-X

Cover design: Joan Dempsey
Cover image: Damir Frkovic/Masterfile

5 6 7 8 - 13 12 11 10
This book is printed on permanent (acid-free) paper ♾.
Printed in Canada

CONTENTS

INTRODUCTION

Good prose, like any art, is part mystery and part technique; both are needed, in varying proportions. Mystery is hard to teach, perhaps impossible. But technique can be taught, and if it is well taught, it can open a window onto the mystery.

This book is not an introduction. I assume that anyone reading it will already have a good grounding in the basics of grammar and style. Although I begin with a few points of grammar, they are only a few, and all of them have some bearing on matters of style. The overall trajectory is from small to large, beginning with words, working up through figures of speech and sentence construction, and ending with the form of large structures, even whole plots. In every case, the discussion is based on real passages from real writers. Some of the passages I think can be improved, in ways I try to illustrate; other passages I admire, for reasons I try to explain.

In a perfect world, there would be no need for editors, but in this world all manuscripts can be improved, and some need a lot of work. When someone expert in a particular field is not so good at putting words together, the editor becomes the essential bridge between the writer's knowledge and the reader's desire to learn. A recent example of an important book flawed by bad writing and insufficient editing is Ian Kershaw's biography of Adolph Hitler.[1] Kershaw's knowledge is encyclopedic, and his interpretation of Hitler's career in the context of German history and society is persuasive. But the many errors of grammar and style in the book are like wrong notes in a symphony, or rotten spots in a peach. Kershaw's book is important; with proper editing, it could have been great.

Some of the editor's job is specialized, but what an editor knows about style a writer should know as well. Creative writers, of course, can often get away with stylistic deviations that would not be welcome in most nonfiction. But these deviations depend on a knowledge of the conventions.

The great experimental writers of the twentieth century were all well trained and knowledgeable; there is no reason to fear that knowledge hinders creativity.

Most professional writers write non-fiction, and most creative writers write non-fiction from time to time. Writers such as Edward Gibbon and Bertrand Russell show that non-fiction can be as just stylish as fiction; in fact, more than a few of the great stylists have been writers of non-fiction. I particularly hope that academic writers, both students and teachers, will find this book useful. Students are supposed to learn how to write from their teachers, but too many academics today write as if they had no interest in making themselves understood. Of course some academic work is specialized, but even specialized work can be well written, and many academic books would find a larger audience if academic writers knew how to write.

My own academic background is in classics, and classical rhetoric is an important theme throughout this book. There are even a few quotations in Greek and Latin, just for fun, but they are all translated, and no knowledge of these languages is required. I do not apologize for including references to the classical tradition. For twenty-five centuries artists and scholars worked to develop a theory of style and composition, and there is still much we can learn from them. The vices of rhetoric can easily be avoided, and in any case they are not the vices that are primarily dangerous for our time.

Before I studied classics I was trained as a musician, and my approach derives as much from the conservatory as from the university. Music education still respects the importance of technique; no one worries that a composer will be harmed by a knowledge of harmony, counterpoint, and formal analysis. The great composers have known what they were doing, and so have the great writers. The evidence is there in the writing, and if we pay attention, we can learn from their work how to improve our own.

A NOTE ON THE EXAMPLES

The examples discussed in this book were not selected according to any plan. They are simply passages I have come across in my reading and have found interesting to think about. They include a good deal of fiction, some history, some literary criticism, some musicology, and a hodge-podge of this and that. A few examples are translations, and in a work of literary criticism these passages might raise legitimate questions of authorship and responsibility: is it the original author or the translator who should take the credit or blame? The goal of this book, however, is analysis, not evaluation, and what matters is the writing as it appears in English, regardless of how it got there.

I have not restricted myself to recent writers, for two reasons. First, I think we can learn from writers of all periods. The principles of good style stay largely the same, though their applications may vary. Second, I fear that our schools, colleges, and universities today, with the best of intentions, offer students too narrow a focus on the present. Of course education should be relevant (whatever that slogan may mean), but it should also be broadening. I learned to read by reading the books I read about in other books, and now a part of my job as a teacher is to point my students toward a larger world, both in space and in time. I hope this book will do the same.

ACKNOWLEDGMENTS

The list of people from whom I have learned is very long. It begins with my parents, Duncan and Mabs Clark, and my sister, Miranda Smith. My teachers in classics have included Richard Crawford, Alexander Dalzell, Michael O'Brien, Richard Thomas, and Richard Tarrant; Gregory Nagy was my dissertation advisor, and his continued support has been most important to me. I studied classical guitar with Sophocles Papas, piano with Boyana Toyich, and composition with Roman Toi. I can't leave out the Split Level Singers: Fred Tippens, Don Doughty, and Bob Bordeaux. Fred and Dodie Tippens (and Sandy and Biffy and Ricky) were my second family when I was in high school. I have spent endless hours talking words and music and painting with Ants Reigo and Laurel Hassell. Doug Freake and Richard Teleky encouraged me at important points during this project. Special thanks are owed to my editor at Oxford, Sally Livingston.

And above all, Reva Marin, to whom this book is dedicated.

A FEW POINTS OF GRAMMAR

Good writers need to be good editors of their own work, and one way to develop editorial skills is to practise editing whatever you happen to read. This book is an attempt to share some of what I have learned over the years from reading other writers. Some of the passages I will discuss are very good, while others—in my opinion—have problems. All these passages are from good writers, including writers I respect and even love. But everyone makes mistakes. This thought is comforting; I know that my own writing is not perfect, hard as I try to do a good job.

Moreover, tastes differ. A passage that I feel has problems may be very much to the taste of another reader. Even so, I hope my discussion will point to issues worth considering. I offer my revisions not as the final answers to the problems at hand, but as suggestions that may lead to other solutions, perhaps better than the ones I have proposed.

A knowledge of grammar—conscious or unconscious—is the foundation of good writing, but it is only the beginning. For the most part my intent in this book is to move beyond grammar to questions of artistry. Still, at the beginning it may be useful to look at a few grammatical problems, to see how even experienced professional writers can sometimes get themselves into trouble.

Almost all writers of non-fiction adhere to the rules codified in the standard grammar texts; so do most fiction writers (most of the time). Prescriptive grammarians sometimes seem to feel that observance of the rules is almost a matter of morality; linguists, on the other hand, point out that the standard is determined partly by social and political forces. I have a foot in each camp. For most purposes, writers are wise to stick to the standard rules, while keeping in mind that "correctness" is not always the most important consideration.

In any event, language changes constantly, and some of the rules learned by one generation may not hold for the next. In modern English, for example, we generally recognize the grammatical function of a word from its position in the sentence. In "The man likes pastrami, but pastrami doesn't like the man," we know that the first "man" is the subject of its clause because it precedes the verb, while the second "man" is the object; and vice versa for "pastrami." A thousand years ago, English was an inflected language and the grammatical function of a word was indicated by its form. Thus the Old English word for "man" was "guma" if it was subject of a clause and "guman" if it was the object. (This Old English word survives in "bridegroom," originally "brydguma.") Because grammatical information was carried by the forms of words, word order was somewhat freer than it is in modern English, though not so free as in ancient Greek, for example.

Pronouns in modern English still change their form: "I like pastrami, but pastrami doesn't like me." Sometimes, especially in speech, we can even move the words around and the grammatical functions will still be clear: "Him, I like." Yet pronouns too are losing some of their inflections. We no longer distinguish between the singular and plural forms of the second-person pronoun (we don't use "thou" anymore), between the subject and object forms ("thou" versus "thee"). These are now dead issues in English grammar.

Still very much alive, however, is the problem of the relative pronoun "who." A hundred years ago, the rule books were unanimous: "who" was the subject form, "whom" the object. Today confusion reigns. In spoken English, "whom" is rare; in writing, some modern grammar books allow "who" as both subject and object; but conservative writers and editors still insist on "whom." In the following passage, from a biography of Benny Goodman, "who" is used as the object of the verb phrase "looking for":

> The Selective Service Draft began in 1940, and as the musicians were exactly the young men who the army was looking for, the draft very quickly began to disrupt the swing bands generally, creating an increasingly competitive scramble for the best men. . . .
>
> James Lincoln Collier, *Benny Goodman and the Swing Era*, 276

The same construction turns up in several other passages (pp. 67, 100, 348). Although I still use "whom" in writing, I can't fault this use of "who." Of course there are ways to avoid the issue altogether: by using "that" instead of "who(m)", or by simply omitting the relative: "young men the army was looking for." What's interesting, however, is that Collier (or his editor) is inconsistent, for some other passages do use "whom":

> Hammond is sometimes given credit for "discovering people" whom he had been tipped off to by other people, but John Chilton, in his biography of Holliday, credits Hammond with this discovery. . . .
>
> James Lincoln Collier, *Benny Goodman and the Swing Era*, 108

Other problems with pronouns are more serious. A fundamental rule of grammar is that any pronoun should have a direct antecedent. This rule is constantly broken in speech, where the context and situation will help make the meaning of the pronoun clear. In writing, however, outside information is usually not available to assist the puzzled reader. Even when it is possible to trace a vague pronoun to its antecedent, in most cases it is better art to spare the reader any unnecessary struggle. Consider the following passage, on the place of rhetoric in Greek tragedy:

> Rhetoric, in short, is counter-dramatic when it is superfluous. This is not always the case. In Medea, for instance, Jason's long, clever, and condemned speech both expounds rhetorically his side of the argument, and simultaneously, displays that shabby personality which is essential to the plot as we have it.
>
> Richmond Lattimore, *Story Patterns in Greek Tragedy*, 67

What is not always the case? That rhetoric is counter-dramatic when it is superfluous? Or that rhetoric is superfluous? I'm sure Lattimore means that rhetoric is not always superfluous, and that when it is not superfluous, it can be dramatic. As the passage is written, readers must hesitate for a moment, because there is no clear antecedent for the pronoun "this." Similar problems often arise with "it," "that," and "which." When revising, it's a good idea to check these words and make sure that the reference is clear.

I hope, by the way, that these two examples prove that I am generally picking on good writers. James Lincoln Collier is one of the very best jazz historians; Richmond Lattimore was an important classical scholar, and perhaps the most influential recent translator of ancient Greek texts into modern English. But everybody makes mistakes.

Here is another example. In this passage Norman Friedman is commenting on Caroline Gordon's interpretation of *A Portrait of the Artist as a Young Man*. Gordon argues that Joyce's novel is not "a picture of the artist rebelling against constituted authority," but "the picture of a soul that is being damned for time and eternity. . . ." Friedman disagrees:

> While I think that this is perverse sophistry, I think also that it is a tribute to Joyce's dramatic genius that a Catholic can sympathize with the portrayal of Catholic values in the novel which the hero rejects.
>
> Norman Friedman, "Point of View in Fiction," in
> Philip Stevick, ed., *Theory of the Novel*, 137

No doubt Friedman means that the hero rejects Catholic values; yet according to the syntax of the sentence, it is the novel which the hero of the novel rejects. The most obvious revision is perhaps a little awkward: "a Catholic can sympathize with the portrayal in the novel of Catholic values which the hero rejects." Is the phrase "in the novel" really necessary? A possessive noun would do just as well: "a Catholic can sympathize with the portrayal of Catholic values which the novel's hero rejects."

Good writing should be more than intelligible. In addition to bare communication there is grace, and grace usually comes from effort. A song sung badly may still be recognizable, though the audience may take no pleasure in the experience; likewise, a bad sentence may make its point, but even expository prose can be graceful. Vague antecedents suggest that the writer simply hasn't taken the time to find the most effective construction.

Here is another example of vague pronoun reference:

> Nor are length, size, or complexity as such criteria of value, though, as we shall see, complexity does have something to do with excellence. Thus, some of Brahms's smaller piano pieces are often considered better works than, for example, his Fourth Symphony. And I am sure that each of us can cite instances of this for himself.
>
> Leonard B. Mayer, *Music, the Arts, and Ideas*, 24

The word "this" in the last sentence lacks a clear antecedent. The general sense of the passage is not hard to deduce: each of us can cite instances of short works that are better than long ones. But does Mayer mean to apply this principle just to the works of Brahms? Or to the works of any single composer? Would a long piece by a poor composer be fairly compared to a short piece by Bach? Because the writing is not precise, these questions are left in the air.

The next passage, from a biography of Giuseppe Verdi, names three people—Emanuele Muzio, Giovanni Ferrari, and Antonio Barezzi—but muddled pronoun references make it hard to tell who is who:

> Emanuele Muzio was born at Zibello in the Duchy of Parma in 1821, the son of the village cobbler. As a boy he studied with Verdi's rival, Ferrari; and when Ferrari moved on in 1840 acted as supply organist of the Collegiate Church. During this time he came under the patronage of Antonio Barezzi, who in 1843, after he had failed to qualify for the priesthood for which he was intended, obtained from the Monte di Pietà a grant to enable him to study music in Milan either at the Conservatory or, if he were refused entry, under a private teacher.

> Julian Budden, *Verdi*, 27

Here is my interpretation of the third sentence: "During this time he [Muzio] came under the patronage of Antonio Barezzi, who [Barezzi] in 1843, after he [Muzio] had failed to qualify for the priesthood for which he [Muzio] was intended, obtained from the Monte di Pietà a grant to enable him [Muzio] to study music in Milan. . . ." If I am right, the second "he" refers to Muzio, but most naturally it ought to refer to "who," which in turn refers to Barezzi. A small survey showed that readers were fairly evenly split on the meaning, but all found the passage confusing.

The next example comes from William Empson, who was one of the most important literary critics and theorists of the twentieth century. His style is often elliptical, even conversational—for good and for bad. There is ease and comfort in his manner, as if he were talking to an old friend, but sometimes he seems to feel that it would not be quite polite to explain what he is talking about. Here, for example, he assumes not only that his readers will know the trombone story, but that they will recognize this Darwin as Erasmus (not Charles). The grammar of this passage is likewise casual, the grammar of conversation:

> There was a period of the cult of Pure Sound when infants were read passages from Homer, and then questioned as to their impressions, not unlike Darwin playing the trombone to his French beans.
>
> William Empson, *Seven Types of Ambiguity*, 11

Comparatives such as "like" or "unlike" require the same kind of construction on each side: X is like Y. The "X" here is complex, but I suppose it reduces to "a period" or, in full, "a period of the cult of Pure Sound." This period is then further described: it was one when infants were read passages from Homer and questioned about their impressions. "Y" then is "Darwin," or "Darwin playing the trombone to his French beans." So "a period of the cult of Pure Sound" is not unlike "Darwin playing the trombone to his French beans." Clearly something has gone wrong.

Another way to approach this problem is to ask what it is that is not unlike Darwin. I think it must be the people who read Homer to infants: the people who read Homer to infants and expected a reaction were just as silly as Darwin when he played the trombone to his beans. (And perhaps we can draw a further conclusion that infants are like French beans.) But the people who did the reading have never been explicitly mentioned—they are the omitted agents of the passive construction—and therefore they cannot be explicitly compared to Darwin. We are left on our own to fill in the blanks.

This passage could be revised fairly easily: "There was a period of the cult of Pure Sound when people read infants passages from Homer, and then questioned them about their impressions, not unlike Darwin playing the trombone to his French beans and looking for a response." Some readers may feel that this revision is not really any better than the original, which is, after all, reasonably clear. Still, I do wish Empson had told us more about Darwin and his beans.

In the next passage a vague "which" leads to a surprising confusion:

> For all her care and delight in place names, to the names of people Jane Austen was surprisingly insensitive. There were, after all, very

few Christian names among her own near relations and those she used over and over again. Not only did she use her own name, which is distinctly unusual—Jane Bennet, Jane Fairfax; she also used her sisters-in-law's names apparently indiscriminately for quite different types of person—"nice" Elizabeth Bennet and "nasty" Elizabeth Elliot, naughty charming Mary Crawford and dull petulant Mary Musgrove.

Marghanita Laski, *Jane Austen and her World*, 52

Here Laski appears to say that Austen's own first name is distinctly unusual. It is of course very common. Most readers will quickly deduce that what is unusual is Austen's habit of giving her own first name to characters in her work. Nevertheless, a small survey showed that while some readers saw no problem, others found the passage almost laughable. I would write: "Not only did she use her own name, a practice which is distinctly unusual...."

An accumulation of pronouns can also lead to confusion, especially if there is a risk of ambiguous reference. In the following passage Emma Woodhouse receives a visit from Frank Churchill and Mrs. Weston:

Emma had hardly expected them: for Mr. Weston, who had called in for half a minute, in order to hear that his son was very handsome, knew nothing of their plans; and it was an agreeable surprise to her, therefore, to perceive them walking up to the house together, arm in arm. She was wanting to see him again; and especially to see him in company with Mrs. Weston, upon his behavior to whom her opinion of him was to depend.

Jane Austen, *Emma*, Chapter 24

Here the second sentence presents us with no fewer than seven pronouns: "she," "him," "him," "his," "whom," "her," and "him." The subject of the sentence is Emma; "him" refers to Frank Churchill; and Emma's opinion of him will depend on his behavior to Mrs. Weston. Although the grammar is technically correct, I found it impossible to understand without effort: "She was wanting to see him again; and especially to see him in company with Mrs. Weston; for his behavior to Mrs. Weston would determine her opinion of him." Even now there is a possible ambiguity: is "her opinion" the opinion of Mrs. Weston, or of Emma herself? I think, however, that the sense is clear.

The dangling modifier is one of the great plagues of sentence construction. Student writers are especially susceptible, but even professionals are not immune:

> Also prominent on the Committee at this time were the authors of the Mundt-Nixon Bill, Karl E. Mundt and Richard M. Nixon. First elected in 1938, and with interests in farming, real estate and insurance, Mundt's hostility to the New Deal, the State Department and the UN helped cement his alliance with McCarthy after he moved from the House to the Senate in January 1949.
>
> David Caute, *The Great Fear*, 91

The second sentence is introduced by a compound adjectival phrase: "First elected in 1938, and with interests in farming, real estate and insurance." Although Caute obviously intends this phrase to describe "Mundt," according to the rule it must modify the subject of the sentence, which is not "Mundt" but "Mundt's hostility." Furthermore, the compound phrase in itself is awkward because its two parts are two different constructions: "first elected in 1938" is a participial phrase, while "with interests in farming, real estate and insurance" is a prepositional phrase. The best solution in this case might be to break the sentence in two: "Mundt, who was first elected in 1938, had interests in farming, real estate and insurance. His hostility to the New Deal, the State Department and the UN helped cement his alliance with McCarthy after he moved from the House to the Senate in January 1949."

Here is another example of a dangling modifier:

> Carson's early and lifelong interest in ornithology was another important source of her love of the natural world. Initiated into birding and bird lore by her mother, the Audubon Society of D.C. . . . enlarged her interest.
>
> Linda Lear, *Rachel Carson: Witness for Nature*, 181

Lear wants to say that Rachel Carson was initiated into birding by her mother; according to the grammar of the sentence, Carson's mother taught the Audubon Society about birds.

Not all dangling modifiers come at the beginning of a sentence. In the next example the problem arises in the middle of the second sentence:

> First rule of the history of science: when a big, new persuasive idea is proposed, an army of critics soon gathers and tries to tear it down. Such a reaction is unavoidable because, aggressive yet abiding by the rules of civil discourse, this is simply how scientists work.

> Edward O. Wilson, *The Diversity of Life*, 26

Wilson means that scientists are aggressive but abide by the rules of scientific discourse; the word "this," however, takes the scientists' place as the subject of the clause. One possible revision might be "Such a reaction is unavoidable because, aggressive yet abiding by the rules of civil discourse, scientists simply work this way." Or, perhaps better, "Such a reaction is unavoidable because this is simply how scientists work; they are aggressive, yet they abide by the rules of civil discourse."

The danger of dangling modifiers is increased by the current habit of beginning a sentence with a modifying phrase or an appositive instead of the subject. Even when the modifier is not dangling, the construction can be awkward. The following is only one of countless possible examples:

> An organized long-term enterprise of discovery, the Portuguese achievement was more modern, more revolutionary than the more widely celebrated exploits of Columbus.

> Daniel Boorstin, *The Discoverers*, 157

The introductory phrase here is not grammatically wrong, but I would still prefer to know from the start what I am reading about: "The Portuguese achievement—an organized long-term enterprise of discovery—was more modern, more revolutionary than the more widely celebrated exploits of Columbus"; or perhaps "Because the Portuguese achievement was an organized long-term enterprise of discovery, it was more modern, more revolutionary than the more widely celebrated exploits of Columbus."

Here is another example of the same construction:

Something of an expert in such matters, Mead had edited and translated texts of the Naassenes and other sects active during the early
years of Christianity.

Noel Stock, The Life of Ezra Pound, 104

There is no particular reason to delay the subject of this sentence. "Mead,
who was something of an expert in such matters...."

Another kind of problem arises when it is not clear where one grammatical construction ends and a second construction begins. In the following passage, it's hard to tell which objects go with which verb:

Low level wastes are produced in large volumes and may require
processing in order to reduce their bulk, storage, and disposal.

Fred Knelman, Nuclear Energy: The Unforgiving Technology, 28

Knelman's point could be that low level wastes "may require processing in
order to reduce (1) their bulk, (2) their storage, and (3) their disposal," but
more likely it is that they "may require (1) processing in order to reduce
their bulk, (2) storage, and (3) disposal." Certainly "bulk" is the direct object
of "reduce." Knelman probably wants "storage" and "disposal" to be direct
objects of "may require," along with "processing," but the reader's first
impulse is to attach those nouns to the verb that most immediately precedes
them: "reduce." A simple change in order helps to clarify the meaning: "Low
level wastes are produced in large volumes and may require storage, disposal, and processing in order to reduce their bulk." This revision, however,
changes the order of the three steps, which Knelman likely arranged in
order of their occurrence. Another possibility is "Low level wastes are produced in large volumes and may require, first, processing in order to reduce
their bulk, and then storage and disposal." Finally, to compound the ambiguity, it is not clear whether the modal verb "may" applies to all three steps
or only the first.

The style books frown on sentence fragments, without condemning
them utterly. In fiction, fragments are particularly common in the sort of
writing often described as poetic prose:

The shadow past is shaped by everything that never happened. Invisible, it melts the present like rain through karst. A biography of longing. It steers us like magnetism, a spirit torque. This is how one becomes undone by a smell, a word, a place, the photo of a mountain of shoes. By love that closes its mouth before calling a name.

I did not witness the most important events of my life. My deepest story must be told by a blind man, a prisoner of sound. From behind a wall, from underground. From the corner of a small house on a small island that juts like a bone from the skin of sea.

Anne Michaels, *Fugitive Pieces*, 17

Fragments can also have a place in non-fiction:

In a future, fully automated age, it may be that the conductor, along with all performing musicians, will be obsolete. Musical creators are working toward that day, assembling electronic scores that, once put on tape, never vary. Which may make the creator happy.

Harold C. Schonberg, *The Great Conductors*, 23–4

In this case, the fragment is essential to the tone of voice that the writer wants the reader to hear. Revision would be an error. The fragment in the next passage, however, breaks the rhythm to no apparent end:

The Elizabethans, for example, were far more widely skilled in the use of metaphor—both in utterance and in interpretation—than we are. A fact which made Shakespeare possible.

I.A. Richards, *The Philosophy of Rhetoric*, 94

If we complete the fragment, we have "This fact made Shakespeare possible"; or, if we change the somewhat colorless word "fact," "This skill made Shakespeare possible." Richards was evidently in a mood when he wrote this passage, for later on the same page we find the following:

Thought is metaphoric, and proceeds by comparison, and the metaphors of language derive therefrom. To improve the theory of metaphor we must remember this. And the method is to take more note of the skill in thought which we possess and are intermittently aware of already. We must translate more of our skill into discussible science. Reflect better upon what we do already so cleverly. Raise our implicit recognitions into explicit distinctions.

> I.A. Richards, *The Philosophy of Rhetoric*, 94–5

Here again the issue is rhythm. I would prefer "We must translate more of our skill into discussible science, reflect better upon what we do already so cleverly, and raise our implicit recognitions into explicit distinctions," but as Richards wrote it the passage has a force that may well have been his goal. I wouldn't have written these fragments, but I'm not sure that as an editor I would change them.

Grammar is not morality, and at times the rules can be broken. It is hardly necessary to cite examples of grammatical deviation in twentieth-century writers such as James Joyce or Gertrude Stein, but even in the nineteenth century some writers sinned for effect. A famous example of characterization through grammatical deviation comes from *The Pickwick Papers*. Mr. Pickwick has quite innocently got himself into a fight with a cab-driver (license number 924), and he is rescued by a man in green coat (later identified as Mr. Jingle):

> "Come along, then," said he of the green coat, lugging Mr. Pickwick after him by main force, and talking the whole way. "Here, No. 924, take your fare, and take yourself off—respectable gentleman—know him well—none of your nonsense—this way, sir—where's your friends?—all a mistake, I see—never mind—accidents will happen—best regulated families—never say die—down upon your luck—pull him up—put that in his pipe—like the flavour—damned rascals." And with a lengthened string of similar broken sentences, delivered with extraordinary volubility, the stranger led the way to the travelers' waiting room, whither he was closely followed by Mr. Pickwick and his disciples.

> Charles Dickens, *The Pickwick Papers*, Chapter 2

And Mark Twain proved that a character can be eloquent even if he doesn't know the schoolbook rules:

You don't know about me without you have read a book by the name of *The Adventures of Tom Sawyer*, but that ain't no matter.

Mark Twain, *The Adventures of Huckleberry Finn*, Chapter 1

William Faulkner often played the narrator's style against the style of his characters in a subtle counterpoint:

Sitting beside the road, watching the wagon mount the hill toward her, Lena thinks, "I have come from Alabama: a fur piece. All the way from Alabama a-walking. A fur piece." Thinking *although I have not been quite a month on the road I am already in Mississippi, further from home than I have ever been before. I am now further from Doane's Mill than I have been since I was twelve years old.*

William Faulkner, *Light in August*, 1

Here the narrator's language follows the rules, while Lena's interior monologue moves from a rural dialect to something close to the narrator's style.

One of the most important trends in recent years is what has come to be called post-colonial literature. Such writing often explores the complex negotiations among different social and political groups in our post-colonial world. Sometimes these negotiations are apparent even in grammar:

I had never see a "coloured" girl in Toronto that look so good and so pretty, and with such a lovely "clear skin," in the three years that I did a student at Trinity College, playing I studying to be a political scientist and the saviour o'Barbados, and then afterwards, when I finish-up at Trinity, bound-'cross the English Channel, enter Middle Temple, tek torts, become a barrister-at-law and gone-back straight home, back to Barbados, to help run the country.

Austin Clarke, "If Only, Only If. . .", from *Nine Men Who Laughed*, 95

Correctness has a value, but there are higher values in art.

🍃

2

THE ARRANGEMENT OF WORDS

So much for grammar. Most of the interesting questions about style do not concern grammar, and do not have definitive answers. They are questions of taste, which can never be settled once and for all. Nevertheless, taste can still be discussed—and, I believe, developed to become more sensitive, more discriminating.

In this chapter we will look at the order and placement of words. In English, word order is relatively fixed: usually the subject comes first, then the verb, which is followed by the object (though there are exceptions). By contrast, languages like Greek or Latin are highly inflected: the grammatical function of a word is marked by its form rather than by its position. As a consequence, these languages allow a great deal of flexibility in word order. The Latin forms "puer" and "puella," meaning "boy" and "girl," are in the nominative case, which is used for the subject of a sentence, while the forms "puerum" and "puellam," also meaning "boy" and "girl," are in the accusative case, which is used for the direct object. So the sentence "Puer amat puellam" and the sentence "Puellam puer amat" mean exactly the same thing—the boy loves the girl—despite the difference in order, and the sentences "Puella amat puerum" and "Puerum puella amat" mean the same thing—the girl loves the boy.

These examples are made-up baby Latin, but real illustrations are not hard to find. The following passage comes from the last book of Homer's *Iliad*, when Priam has come to ask Achilles for the body of Hector. Although there is a great deal of tension in this encounter, the two heroic enemies look at each other with admiration:

ἤτοι Δαρδανίδης Πρίαμος θαύμαζ᾽ Ἀχιλῆα,

ὅσσος ἔην οἷός τε· θεοῖσι γὰρ ἄντα ἐῴκει·

αὐτὰρ ὁ Δαρδανίδην Πρίαμον θαύμαζεν Ἀχιλλεύς,
εἰσορόων ὄψίν τ' ἀγαθὴν καὶ μῦθον ἀκούων.

Il.24.629-632

Truly Dardanian Priam wondered at Achilles,
how great and handsome he was; for he was like the gods to look at.
But Achilles wondered at Dardanian Priam
looking at his beautiful face and hearing his words.

In the first sentence the words Δαρδανίδης Πριαμος (Dardanian Priam) are in the nominative case and function as the subject of the clause; in the third line the same words (Δαρδανίδην Πρίαμον) are in the accusative case and function as the object, even though they have retained their position in the line. Conversely, the name of Achilles at the end of the first line is accusative, but at the end of the third line it is nominative. The English translation here changes the order of the words to retain their grammatical functions. Another solution would be to keep the order of the words but change the voice of the verb, from active in the first line ("Dardanian Priam wondered at Achilles") to passive in the third ("Dardanian Priam was wondered at by Achilles").

Order in English is certainly not as flexible as it is in Greek or Latin, but there are points of flexibility, particularly in the placement of qualifying expressions such as adverbs and adverbial phrases:

In a recent novel a lady makes one of her characters clatter up to take part in a very poignant scene in a motor car.

Edwin Muir, *The Structure of the Novel*, 118

Presumably Muir means that the character clatters up in a motor car, not that the poignant scene takes place in one. The prepositional phrase has been misplaced.

A similar problem mars the following passage, from R. Blackmur's discussion of Thomas Hardy:

In this poem and others of its class, Hardy obtains objective and self-sufficient strength precisely by *reducing* his private operative means to a minimum, by getting rid of or ignoring most of the machinery he ordinarily used altogether.

R. Blackmur, *Form and Value in Modern Poetry*, 12

Here the adverb "altogether" is too far from the word it qualifies. To my ear it would make more sense to say that "Hardy obtains . . . strength precisely by *reducing* his private operative means to a minimum, by altogether getting rid of or ignoring most of the machinery he ordinarily used." Or perhaps the following is better yet: ". . . by ignoring or altogether getting rid of most of the machinery he ordinarily used."

Adverbs and adverbial phrases tend to follow the verbs they modify. When several of them pile up at the end of a sentence, they can hobble the rhythm and give it a rather lumbering quality:

Among the most popular novels ever written is Mrs. Susanah Rowson's *Charlotte Temple: A Tale of Truth*, first published in 1791 and reprinted in more than 160 editions in the century that followed in the United States alone.

Philip Stevick, *The Chapter in Fiction*, 105

This sentence ends with four prepositional phrases—(1) "in 1791," (2) "in more than 160 editions," (3) "in the century that followed," (4) "in the United States alone"—and the last three run together in a single sequence. A simple revision will group the two temporal phrases together, leaving only two phrases to follow the verb "reprinted": "Among the most popular novels ever written is Mrs. Susanah Rowson's *Charlotte Temple: A Tale of Truth*, first published in 1791, and in the century that followed reprinted in more than 160 editions in the United States alone."

These examples suggest two general principles: first, that words which function as a group should usually be placed reasonably close together; second, that the end of a sentence is a position of some importance. The following sentence illustrates the first of these principles:

But such a projection of identity into the identity of others for someone like Moll who compulsively fears losing control of her identity is not an easy thing.

William J. Krier, "A Courtesy which Grants Integrity: A Literal
Reading of Moll Flanders," *ELH*, September 1971, 402-3

Here the subject is so far away from the predicate that the reader is likely
to forget what it was by the end of the sentence. That subject is fairly complex in itself, and could probably be clarified simply by dropping one of its
two "identities": "a projection into the identity of others." The real problem, however, is the placement of the long prepositional phrase, with its
attached relative clause: "for someone like Moll who compulsively fears
losing control of her identity." If that phrase is moved from the middle of
the sentence to the beginning, the structure becomes clear: "But for someone like Moll, who compulsively fears losing control of her identity, such a
projection into the identity of others is not an easy thing."

Another example comes from Northrop Frye:

> To bring my own view that criticism as knowledge should constantly
> progress and reject nothing into direct experience would mean that
> the latter should progress toward a general stupor of satisfaction with
> everything written, which is not quite what I had in mind.
>
> Northrop Frye, *The Anatomy of Criticism*, 28

The prepositional phrase "into direct experience" is too far away from its
verb ("bring"), so that it appears to modify the intervening phrase "should
. . . reject nothing." Although the proper relationships can be deduced, the
reader is likely to suffer a momentary confusion, and in any case the effect
is inelegant—though the ending of the sentence is quite lovely. Here are
two possible revisions:

> To bring my own view—that criticism as knowledge should constantly
> progress and reject nothing—into direct experience would mean that
> the latter should progress toward a general stupor of satisfaction with
> everything written, which is not quite what I had in mind.

> To bring into direct experience my own view—that criticism as
> knowledge should constantly progress and reject nothing—would
> mean that the latter should progress toward a general stupor of satisfac-
> tion with everything written, which is not quite what I had in mind.

Perhaps, however, a more extensive revision is necessary. Frye has attempted to do rather a lot in this sentence. First, he has described his own view—that criticism as knowledge should constantly progress and reject nothing. Second, he has suggested that this view could be brought into direct experience—presumably making a distinction between critical theory and the actual practice of reading. Third, he has remarked on a consequence of bringing his view into direct experience: experience would progress toward a general stupor of satisfaction with everything written. And, finally, he has given his judgment of this putative consequence: it is not what he had in mind. A sentence with so much to do is likely to run into some problems. Perhaps it should be divided: "My own view is that criticism as knowledge should constantly progress and reject nothing. But to bring that view into direct experience would mean that experience would progress toward a general stupor of satisfaction with everything written, which is not quite what I had in mind."

Another passage from the same work illustrates the principle that the end of a sentence is a position of some importance:

> The critic is in the position of a mathematician who has to deal with numbers so large that it would keep him scribbling digits until the next ice age even to write them out in their conventional form as integers.
>
> Northrop Frye, *The Anatomy of Criticism*, 16

In the previous examples, the word or phrase at the end of the sentence has been too far from the words it belongs with; here, the word groupings are clear: "as integers" goes properly with "in their conventional form", which in turn goes properly with "to write them out." Nonetheless the statement falls flat at the end. The reason, I think, is that Frye has chosen to use the dummy form "it" in the subject position—"it would keep him scribbling digits . . ."—and as a result has passed up a chance to build suspense as the sentence progresses. There is nothing wrong with using a dummy subject, especially when it offers a way around an awkward construction. In this case, however, there is no reason not to use the real subject—"to write them out in their conventional form as integers"—in the subject position, so that the strong point can come at the end: "The critic is in the position of a mathematician who has to deal with numbers so large that even to write them out in their conventional form as integers would keep him scribbling digits until the next ice age."

The next passage is very vivid, but I wonder whether the ending could be improved:

> In a dark corner of the chapel at the gospel side of the altar a stout old lady knelt amid her copious black skirts. When she stood up a pink dressed figure, wearing a curly golden wig and an old fashioned straw sun-bonnet, with black pencilled eyebrows and delicately rouged and powdered, was discovered.
>
> James Joyce, *A Portrait of the Artist as a Young Man*, 74

The end of the second sentence seems something of a letdown. Perhaps the verb can be brought forward. Several revisions are possible. An observer could be introduced; this change would have the added benefit of changing the passive "was discovered" to the active: "When she stood up, one could see a pink dressed figure. . . ." If "one" is too weak, perhaps "When she stood up, Stephen saw. . . ." But presumably Joyce had a reason for keeping Stephen out of the scene, so perhaps it is over-bold to introduce him. A reflexive verb would eliminate the observer and keep the reader's eye on the old lady: "When she stood up, she revealed herself as a pink dressed figure, wearing a curly golden wig and an old fashioned straw sun-bonnet, with black pencilled eyebrows and delicately rouged and powdered."

Complex sentences raise complex questions of word order and emphasis. Generally the most important ideas of a sentence are carried by the main clause, the less important by one or more subordinate clauses. In turn, within each of these clauses, new questions of order and emphasis arise. In the following passage Johan Huizinga is discussing the mystical symbolism of the late Middle Ages:

> The Breton, Alain de la Roche, a Dominican, born about 1428, is a very typical representative of this religious imagery, both ultra-concrete and ultra-fantastic. He was the zealous promoter of the use of the rosary, with a view to which he founded the Universal Brotherhood of the Psalter of Our Lady. The description of his numerous visions is characterized at the same time by an excess of sexual imagination and by the absence of all genuine emotion. The

passionate tone which, in the grand mystics, makes these too sensuous images of hunger and thirst, of blood and voluptuousness, bearable, is altogether lacking.

> J. Huizinga, *The Waning of the Middle Ages*, translated by
> F. Hopman, 191

The final sentence of this passage consists of two clauses. The main clause says that a passionate tone is lacking in Alain's imagery, and the second identifies this passionate tone as the element that makes overly sensuous images in the grand mystics bearable. These images are further specified as images of hunger and thirst, blood and voluptuousness. Which ideas should be emphasized? Which should be the main clause and which the subordinate? Within each clause, which order of words will work best? Many different arrangements of this complex sentence are possible, and each has a different feeling.

"The passionate tone which makes these too sensuous images of hunger and thirst, of blood and voluptuousness bearable in the grand mystics, is altogether lacking." This first revision keeps "lacking" at the end of the main clause, but it rearranges the subordinate clause.

A second revision completes the main clause before starting on the subordinate clause, which takes an increased emphasis from its new position: "The passionate tone is altogether lacking, which, in the grand mystics, makes these too sensuous images of hunger and thirst, of blood and voluptuousness, bearable."

A third revision changes the order of words in the subordinate clause, in order to emphasize the description of the images: "The passionate tone is altogether lacking, which, in the grand mystics, makes bearable these too sensuous images of hunger and thirst, of blood and voluptuousness."

A fourth revision reorders the beginning of the subordinate clause: "The passionate tone is altogether lacking which makes bearable, in the grand mystics, these too sensuous images of hunger and thirst, of blood and voluptuousness."

And a fifth revision rearranges the words in the subordinate clause, but keeps the end of the main clause at the end of the sentence: "The passionate tone which, in the grand mystics, makes bearable these too sensuous images of hunger and thirst, of blood and voluptuousness, is altogether lacking."

My own preference is for the last version. The important point, however, is the number of arrangements that are possible and the differences of emphasis in each case; which is best is a matter of personal judgment.[1]

When I first read the following sentence, I was quite confused:

> The difficulty that I felt in being quite composed that first evening, when Ada asked me, over our work, if the family were at the house, and when I was obliged to answer yes, I believed so, for Lady Dedlock had spoken to me in the woods the day before yesterday, was great.

> Charles Dickens, *Bleak House*, Chapter 37

Clearly the verb phrase "was great" is too far from its subject. Revision here is not difficult, though there is more than one possibility:

> The difficulty that I felt in being quite composed was great, that first evening, when Ada asked me, over our work, if the family were at the house, and when I was obliged to answer yes, I believed so, for Lady Dedlock had spoken to me in the woods the day before yesterday.

> That first evening—when Ada asked me over our work, if the family were at the house, and I was obliged to answer yes, I believed so, for Lady Dedlock had spoken to me in the woods the day before yesterday—the difficulty that I felt in being quite composed was great.

If the last clause of this version—"the difficulty that I felt in being quite composed was great"—seems unnecessarily complex, perhaps it could be replaced by "I felt great difficulty in being quite composed" or "I could hardly keep composed."

The end of a sentence or clause is not the only possible locus of trouble:

> Our inner life is a complex of religious aspirations, fears, struggles to survive in an environment which at times is hostile and at others friendly, illusions, images and fictions.

> George Boas, Preface to Johann Jakob Bachofen, *Myth, Religion and Mother Right*, xii

Boas here is making a list. Most of the items in the list are single terms, but one is complex. By placing the complex item in the middle, he has constructed a sentence that is potentially confusing and certainly awkward. Revision is simple: "Our inner life is a complex of religious aspirations, fears, illusions, images, fictions, and struggles to survive in an environment which at times is hostile and at others friendly." This example illustrates the law of increasing numbers: generally speaking, items in a series should be arranged in order of increasing length or importance.

Improper placement of a negative word can be particularly confusing:

> No more than Maimonides, St. Thomas Aquinas was inclined to mistake religiosity for religion.
>
> Etienne Gilson, *The Unity of Philosophical Experience*, 48

The main clause here says that St. Thomas was inclined to mistake religiosity for religion—the opposite of what Gilson wanted to say. The confusion arises because the negative has been placed in an introductory phrase. A simple rearrangement solves the problem: "St. Thomas Aquinas was no more inclined than Maimonides to mistake religiosity for religion."

The difficulties caused by improper placement of the negative increase if the construction is long or complicated. The next passage concerns Eugene Rostow, a neo-conservative politician of the 1960s and '70s, and Eugene Debs, the leader of the US Socialist party in the early years of the twentieth century. In the second sentence, "not" belongs with "because," but the two are separated by 22 words and a couple of clauses:

> Many so-called neo-conservatives share with Rostow a youthful commitment to idealistic socialism, a commitment they have long since repudiated but which they still recall with feelings of great bitterness. Rostow, for example, was not named Eugene Victor Debs Rostow by his father and mother—who, as he told me, met at a socialist rally in Brooklyn—because they wanted him to grow up to be a neo-conservative.
>
> Robert Scheer, *With Enough Shovels*, 47

A simple revision would put the negative where it belongs: "Rostow's parents, for example—who, as he told me, met at a socialist rally in Brooklyn—named him Eugene Victor Debs Rostow not because they wanted him to grow up to be a neo-conservative." But the sentence still sounds awkward and over-complicated. Another revision would cut it in two: "Rostow, for example, told me that his parents met at a socialist rally in Brooklyn. If they named him Eugene Victor Debs, it was not because they wanted him to grow up to be a neo-conservative."

A double negative in literary English equals a positive. In many dialects of English, however, this construction is simply an emphatic negative: "I don't want no trouble from you." The distinction has become a marker of class and education, but the logical argument against this emphatic construction is not strong. In ancient Greek, for example, emphatic double and even triple or quadruple negatives are common; and any construction that Plato used can't be all wrong. Nonetheless, in formal contexts two negatives make a positive, and a careful writer will make it easy for readers to keep track of the addition:

> We now know that both Abraham and Homer had predecessors, and we have good grounds for suspecting that these predecessors were in some sort of contact with each other. Archaeology shows that there was not a century of the Iron Age during which Greek artifacts, mostly ceramics, were not being brought into Syria and Palestine.
>
> Moses Hadas, *Hellenistic Culture*, 6

Here two negatives are deployed without confusion, because the second negative is placed properly near its verb and because the rhythm of the sentence allows it to be heard emphatically. The next example, however, from Frank Kermode, I find incomprehensible.

This passage comes in the course of a discussion of time. Kermode, following the Christian theologian John Marsh,[2] uses two Greek words to distinguish two kinds of time: *chronos* signifies the ordinary time that passes, *kairos* the time that is a moment of special crisis or significance, time charged with meaning. According to James Barr, however, the distinction between *chronos* and *kairos* cannot be found in the New Testament. Here Kermode argues that Barr's critique goes even further:

> Mr. Barr's authoritative book contains much more destructive criticism than this suggests. Among other things, it discourages too easy

acceptance of sharp distinctions between Christian rectilinearity and Greek cyclicalism. But the main issue here is that Barr makes it impossible for anybody who is not willing to engage him on his own lexical terms to doubt that Marsh's distinction, which I have used, can have any very certain validity.

Frank Kermode, *The Sense of an Ending*, 49

The last sentence has only one "not," but since "impossible" and "doubt" are negative as well, the cumulative effect is at least a triple negative. I have no idea what this sentence means. Perhaps it would help to break the sentence down to its simplest elements and then gradually add the complicating structures.

(1) "Marsh's distinction [i.e., the distinction between *chronos* and *kairos*] has validity."

(2) "I doubt that Marsh's distinction can have any very certain validity."

(3) "It is possible to doubt that Marsh's distinction can have any very certain validity."

(4) "It is not possible to doubt that Marsh's distinction can have any very certain validity." Here, I think, the trouble begins. This sentence is the negation of the previous proposition (number 3). It should mean "One must believe that Marsh's distinction has validity"— "not" and "doubt" cancel out and make the sentence overall a positive assertion. If so, the use of "any" in proposition four is not correct. I would not say "One must believe that Marsh's distinction has any validity"; I would say "One must believe that Marsh's distinction has some validity." In the same way, I would say "I want some sugar" but "I don't want any sugar." The use of "any" here requires that the whole construction have a negative sense.[3]

(5) "Barr makes it impossible for anybody to doubt that Marsh's distinction can have any very certain validity." That is, "Because of Barr's argument, one must believe that Marsh's distinction has validity."

(6) "Barr makes it impossible for anybody who is willing to engage him on his own lexical terms to doubt that Marsh's distinction can have any very certain validity." This sentence would mean that because of what Barr says, anybody who is willing to engage him on his own lexical terms must believe that Marsh's distinction has some validity. In other

words, those people who are willing to engage him on his own lexical terms ought to believe that Marsh's distinction has some validity. I think that "him" and "his own" refer to Barr.

(7) "Barr makes it impossible for anybody who is not willing to engage him on his own lexical terms to doubt that Marsh's distinction can have any very certain validity." This stage of analysis is the same as Kermode's original, lacking only the introductory "But the main issue here is that" and the parenthetical "which I have used." If my reading of the previous proposition is correct, this sentence should mean that, because of Barr's argument, those people who are not willing to engage him on his own lexical terms ought to believe that Marsh's distinction has some validity. I am not at all sure, however, that this is what Kermode meant to say.

The thinking of Henry James is usually complex and often ambiguous; he was interested in fine discriminations of feeling, and the structure of his sentences often follows the structure of those discriminations. In the following passage, from the beginning of *The Wings of the Dove*, Kate Croy has come to see her father. The end of the passage contrasts the feelings of father and daughter. Each wants to see the other, though Mr. Croy's desire is heavily qualified. Kate's feelings are perhaps even more complex. She wants to see her father, but she knows that the experience will be painful:

> When her father at last appeared she became, as usual, instantly aware of the futility of any effort to hold him to anything. He had written her that he was ill, too ill to leave his room, and that he must see her without delay; and if this had been, as was probable, the sketch of a design, he was indifferent even to the moderate finish required for deception. He had clearly wanted, for perversities that he called reasons, to see her, just as she herself had sharpened for a talk; but now she felt again, in the inevitability of the freedom he used with her, all the old ache, her poor mother's very own, that he couldn't touch her ever so lightly without setting up.
>
> Henry James, *The Wings of the Dove*, Chapter 1

At first glance, the ending of this passage might seem too weak to carry the weight of the emotions expressed. The emphasis might better fall on "ache" or "touch" or, perhaps best, "ever so lightly." But revision is not easy. The best I could contrive would be to change the negative "without setting up" into a positive: "but now she felt again, in the inevitability of the freedom he used with her, all the old ache, her poor mother's very own, that was always [or inescapably] set up by his touch, no matter how light." With James, however, even a minor change can amount to major surgery. In the original, the negative elements—"couldn't," "without"—help to create a feeling of simultaneous attraction and withdrawal. The revision not only loses the negative but changes an active construction, in which the father himself reaches out to touch, to a passive one involving only a disembodied hand: "was set up by his touch." It could even be argued that the original ending—"ever so lightly without setting up"—is exquisitely effective, with the "up" at the end producing an almost palpable tiny shock. The difficulty of improving this sentence by rearrangement shows how delicate an organism it is.

3

RHYTHM

Metrics, as the name suggests, is the measurement of rhythm. Rhythm itself is rather hard to define; as they say, if you have to ask what it is, you'll never know. Metrical analysis can sometimes feel like trying to catch moonlight in a bottle. Still, we make do the best we can with the tools we have.[1]

The terminology of metrics was developed in the ancient world to deal with Greek and Latin verse. In these languages what counts is the length of a syllable, and different combinations of long and short syllables form different units called feet. Although English verse is based on stress—strong syllables versus weak syllables—we still call the various feet by their classical names, which I will list in a moment. The standard symbol for a strong or stressed syllable is a sloping line; for a weak or unstressed syllable, a symbol shaped sort of like the letter "U." Most English verse can be described with just six different feet:

iamb	weak, strong	U /
trochee	strong, weak	/ U
dactyl	strong, weak, weak	/ U U
anapest	weak, weak, strong	U U /
spondee	strong, strong	/ /
pyrrhic	weak, weak	U U

If we use this system to describe prose rhythm, we need to add to the list:

amphibrach	weak, strong, weak	U / U
cretic	strong, weak, strong	/ U /
bacchic	weak, strong, strong	U / /
mollosus	strong, strong, strong	/ / /
tribrach	weak, weak, weak	U U U
antipast	weak, strong, strong, weak	U / / U

choriamb	strong, weak, weak, strong	/ U U /
ionic a majore	strong, strong, weak, weak	/ / U U
ionic a minore	weak, weak, strong, strong	U U / /

In addition, the epitrite has any of the various combinations of one weak and three strong syllables, while the paeon has any of the various combinations of one strong and three weak syllables. The very rare foot with a single syllable is sometimes called a monometer.

The first scholar to discuss prose rhythm was Aristotle. In Chapter 3, section 8, of his *Art of Rhetoric*, he argues that prose is different from verse; it should have rhythm, he says, but not a strict meter. He goes on to characterize the most common feet: the dactyl is grand and heroic, the trochee more like a comic dance. The iamb is closest to normal conversation, while the paeon is good because it attracts the least notice. For the beginning of a sentence, he recommends one strong and three weak syllables; for the end, three weak and one strong.

Some 250 years later, Cicero elaborated on Aristotle's method of metrical analysis, paying particular attention to metrical patterns, especially at the ends of his sentences.[2] And through Cicero this method was transmitted to the Renaissance critics and almost down to our own time.

The most assiduous scholar of the subject in English is George Saintsbury, whose *History of English Prose Rhythm* offers hundreds of detailed metrical analyses of passages from Anglo-Saxon through Middle English and Early Modern English and down to the beginning of the twentieth century. Saintsbury's own style, however, is often not very good, and it is therefore difficult to trust either his analysis or his judgment of other writers. Here are a few sentences from the beginning of his book:

> That it is possible, and not undesirable, to consider prose almost as curiously as verse itself, is a . . . contentious proposition. It is, however, certain, on the one hand, that, in the very dawn of criticism, Aristotle, who threw light on many things, practically started the whole inquiry in which this book is an essay, by his description of prose as "neither possessing metre nor destitute of rhythm"; and that, in this context of the Rhetoric, he discussed Greek prose scansion with some fullness. It is equally certain that this distinction—one of those which commend themselves, as soon as proposed, to almost

every intelligence—was followed, though not probably to any very great extent, by critics both Greek and Latin. And we possess, in particular, a consideration of Latin prose rhythm by Quintilian, which forms a not unworthy pendant to Aristotle's in regard to Greek.

> George Saintsbury, *A History of English Prose Rhythm*, 1–2

The jerky rhythm of the second sentence, with its succession of short phrases, is typical of Saintsbury's style.

The metrical method of analysis, as Saintsbury applies it, breaks prose into short feet, though exactly how these divisions are established he never explains. Some of his examples seem to suggest that a foot consists of one strong syllable and its weak neighbors, but in other passages he allows feet with more than one strong syllable. Here, for example, is his scansion of a passage by Sir William Temple, a seventeenth-century English diplomat and essayist:[3]

> When áll | is dóne, | húman | lífe | ís, | at the greátest | and the bést, | but líke | a fróward | chíld | that must be pláyed with | and húmoured | a líttle | to keép it | quíet | till it fálls | asleép; | and thén | the cáre | is óver.

> Saintsbury, *A History of English Prose Rhythm,* 237

In technical terms, Saintsbury's scansion is iamb, iamb, trochee, monometer, monometer, paeon, anapest, iamb, amphibrach . . . and so on. Since this is prose, we don't expect a regular pattern, but this analysis is just a jumble that explains nothing. Moreover, the division into short feet gives an oddly disjointed impression of the rhythm, in this passage and all the others he analyzes. I would read the passage this way:

> When áll is dóne, | húman lífe ís, | at the greátest and the bést, | but líke a fróward chíld | that must be pláyed with | and húmoured a líttle | to keép it quíet till it fálls asleép; | and thén the cáre is óver.

This analysis divides the sentence into only eight parts, instead of twenty. Each part is rhythmically different, and this variety keeps the ear interested. The first four parts all end on stressed syllables; then the rhythm becomes less marked, the divisions lengthen, and a regular iambic movement, ending on an unstressed syllable, brings the sentence to a tranquil close. A change in the speed of the reading might shift a few of the stresses, and the phrase "played with and humoured a little" could perhaps remain undivided. In any case, my analysis is based on rhythm as an interaction of meter, grammatical structure, and meaning. In general, breaks come at the boundaries of grammatical constituents, especially where those boundaries mark a clear progress in the meaning of the sentence. I think this is the most natural way to think about the divisions of a prose sentence.[4]

The metrical approach to prose is probably useful for the beginnings and endings of sentences, since it provides a set of terms we can use to describe and compare passages. I am not sure, however, that a theory of prose rhythm is possible. There are too many good rhythms, and too many factors involved in the creation of rhythm. In addition to the distribution of stressed and unstressed syllables, one has to consider the lengths of words, phrases, clauses, and sentences; the effects of balance and repetition; the tone of voice and the speed appropriate to the passage; and also the rhythm of the thought. As a general principle, good prose sounds good when it is read aloud. But there are many ways of sounding good.

The following passage, from the very beginning of *Mansfield Park*, shows one kind of good rhythm:

> About thirty years ago, Miss Maria Ward, of Huntingdon, with only seven thousand pounds, had the good luck to captivate Sir Thomas Bertram, of Mansfield Park, in the county of Northampton, and to be thereby raised to the rank of a baronet's lady, with all the comforts and consequences of an handsome house and large income. All Huntingdon exclaimed on the greatness of the match, and her uncle, the lawyer, himself allowed her to be at least three thousand pounds short of any equitable claim to it. She had two sisters to be benefited by her elevation; and such of their acquaintances as thought Miss Ward and Miss Frances quite as handsome as Miss Maria, did not scruple to predict their marrying with almost equal advantage. But there certainly are not so many men of large fortune in the world as there are pretty women to deserve them.

Jane Austen, Mansfield Park, Chapter 1

Many of the phrases are short, but the lengths are varied, and the passage reads easily, with no feeling of breathlessness. Each sentence swells towards a climax, and the passage as a whole ends with an ironic summation, the only sentence in the passage that is not broken into sections:

About thirty years ago,
Miss Maria Ward,
of Huntingdon,
with only seven thousand pounds,
had the good luck to captivate Sir Thomas Bertram,
of Mansfield Park,
in the county of Northampton,
and to be thereby raised to the rank of a baronet's lady,
with all the comforts and consequences of an handsome house and
    large income.
All Huntingdon exclaimed on the greatness of the match,
and her uncle,
the lawyer,
himself allowed her to be at least three thousand pounds short of any
    equitable claim to it.
She had two sisters to be benefited by her elevation;
and such of their acquaintances as thought Miss Ward and Miss
    Frances quite as handsome as Miss Maria,
did not scruple to predict their marrying with almost equal advantage.
But there certainly are not so many men of large fortune in the
    world as there are pretty women to deserve them.

The overall effect is cool, controlled, informative, and intelligent. This is good rhythm, but it is by no means the only way of being good. The following passage has some of the same ironic detachment, but with a very different set of rhythmic effects:

The station wagons arrived at noon, a long shining line that coursed through the west campus. In single file they eased around the orange I-beam sculpture and moved toward the dormitories. The roofs of the station wagons were loaded down with carefully secured suit-cases full of light and heavy clothing; with boxes of blankets, boots and shoes, stationery and books, sheets, pillows, quilts; with rolled-up rugs and sleeping bags; with bicycles, skis, rucksacks, English and Western saddles, inflated rafts. As cars slowed to a crawl and stopped, students sprang out and raced to the rear doors to begin removing the objects inside; the stereo sets, radios, personal computers; small refrigerators and table ranges; the cartons of phonograph records and cassettes; the hairdryers and styling irons; the tennis rackets, soccer balls, hockey and lacrosse sticks, bows and arrows; the controlled substances, the birth control pills and devices; the junk food still in shopping bags—onion-and-garlic chips, nacho thins, peanut creme patties, Waffelos and Kabooms, fruit chews and toffee popcorn; the Dum-Dum pops, the Mystic mints.

I've witnessed this spectacle every September for twenty-one years. It is a brilliant event, invariably. The students greet each other with comic cries and gestures of sodden collapse. Their summer has been bloated with criminal pleasures, as always. The parents stand sun-dazed near their automobiles, seeing images of themselves in every direction. The conscientious suntans. The well-made faces and wry looks. They feel a sense of renewal, of communal recognition. The women crisp and alert, in diet trim, knowing people's names. Their husbands content to measure out the time, distant but ungrudging, accomplished in parenthood, something about them suggesting massive insurance coverage. This assembly of station wagons, as much as anything they might do in the course of the year, more than formal liturgies or laws, tells the parents they are a collection of the like-minded and the spiritually akin, a people, a nation.

Don DeLillo, *White Noise*, 3–4

Part of the effect here is created by the careful balance of longer and shorter phrases, as well as rhythmic variation created by the lengths of different words and word combinations. At the beginning, there are four longish phrases, which seem to read best with no strong internal divisions:

The station wagons arrived at noon,
a long shining line that coursed through the west campus.
In single file they eased around the orange I-beam sculpture and

moved toward the dormitories.
The roofs of the station wagons were loaded down with carefully
   secured suitcases full of light and heavy clothing;

But now the passage moves to a series of short phrases:

with boxes of blankets, boots and shoes,
stationery and books,
sheets, pillows, quilts;
with rolled-up rugs and sleeping bags;
with bicycles, skis, rucksacks,
English and Western saddles,
inflated rafts.

These short phrases have been carefully varied so that no two have quite
the same rhythm; although both "sheet, pillows, quilts" and "inflated rafts"
have four syllables, the distribution of stresses is very different. There are also
delicate hints of alliteration.

Much of this passage is taken up with a careful catalogue of objects, personal possessions; the rhetorical term for a heap of words is congeries. In
modern style, long sentences are often simply lists, with little grammatical
complication. Here I think the effect is to suggest that these people live
through their possessions. Many of the items have an air of indulgence and
frivolity, which is reinforced by the insistent rhythm.

Towards the end of the passage, the sentence fragments add a different
rhythm:

The parents stand sun-dazed near their automobiles,
seeing images of themselves in every direction.
The conscientious suntans.
The well-made faces and wry looks.
They feel a sense of renewal, of communal recognition.
The women crisp and alert,
in diet trim,
knowing people's names.
Their husbands content to measure out the time,
distant but ungrudging,

accomplished in parenthood,
something about them suggesting massive insurance coverage.

The characterizations of the women and their husbands are roughly parallel, but varied, and the general increase in length adds to the sense of climax; the rhythm reinforces the satiric tone of "massive insurance coverage." Finally, like Austen in the passage from *Mansfield Park*, DeLillo concludes with an ironic summation. Here, however, two short phrases reinforce the ironic climax:

This assembly of station wagons,
as much as anything they might do in the course of the year,
more than formal liturgies or laws,
tells the parents they are a collection of like-minded and the spiri-
    tually akin,
a people,
a nation.

Because there are so many good styles, so many good rhythms, no passage, no group of passages, can be an adequate or reliable model. As good as Austen is, she is not good in the way DeLillo is good; and neither is good in the way that Saul Bellow is, or Faulkner or Fielding. Of course studying the rhythms of good writers can increase awareness and sensitivity. For those of us seeking to improve our own writing, however, analysis of failure is often more instructive.

The following passage has, to my ear, the same problem we saw in Saintsbury, where the natural units of structure and sense were broken up by needless interruptions:

We must therefore accept, unless we may have accumulated sufficient reasons to doubt, Moll's explanation for her "thorough aver-
sion to going to service," with which she, when pressed by her
nurse, provides us.

William J. Krier, "A Courtesy Which Grants Integrity: A Literal
Reading of *Moll Flanders*," *ELH*, Sept. 1971, 398

The first clause is "we must therefore accept . . . Moll's explanation"—subject, verb, and direct object. But this natural grammatical unit has been interrupted by the parenthetical "unless we have accumulated sufficient reasons to doubt." This phrase could easily come first. Then the second clause— "with which she provides us"—is likewise interrupted by the phrase "when pressed by her nurse." Here some interruption is perhaps inescapable—and of course there is no absolute rule against it. My ear, however, prefers the parenthesis after "which" rather than after "she":

> Unless we may have accumulated sufficient reasons to doubt it, we must therefore accept Moll's explanation for her "thorough aversion to going to service," which, when pressed by her nurse, she provides us.

Rhythm includes not only the run of the words in the sentence, but also the structure of thought in the sentence and in the passage as a whole. The flow of sense can be impeded by words that have little meaning or function. Excessive qualification—hedging and dodging—can lead to excess words and bad rhythm:

> Those who read me know my conviction that the world, the temporal world, rests on a few very simple ideas: so simple that they must be as old as the hills. It rests, notably, among others, on the idea of Fidelity.

> Joseph Conrad, preface to *A Personal Record*

The last sentence of this passage should drive straight on to its conclusion—the idea of Fidelity—but its progress is hampered by commas. The same qualification can be made with fewer words and no interruption: "First among these is the idea of Fidelity" or "Notable among these is. . . ." The repetition of "rests" is lost; but "me/my," "the world/the temporal world," "simple/simple," "idea/ideas" are perhaps repetition enough.

Here is another example of excessive qualification:

> Metaphor, then, would seem to be, very commonly at least, the outcome of an emotional mood reacting, as such a mood generally does, on the imagination.

> Stephen J. Brown, S.J., *The World of Imagery*, 54

Is so much qualification necessary? I can understand the impulse not to say more than one means, but here the single word "often" before the verb seems sufficient: "Metaphor, then, would often seem to be the outcome of an emotional mood reacting on the imagination."

The next passage begins with a universal claim, which the authors then abandon:

> All art is traditional in that artists learn their craft from their predecessors to a great extent.
>
> Robert Scholes and Robert Kellogg, *The Nature of Narrative*, 4

It would be better to start with more restraint; then the hedging would not be necessary, and the sentence could end with strong semantic weight: "Art in general is traditional, in that artists learn their craft from their predecessors"; or "Art is traditional, in that artists generally learn their craft from their predecessors."

The phrase "the fact that" can almost always be cut, although some grammatical reorganization will be required:

> The greatest obstacle to recognizing the expressive value of rhetorical devices is the fact that they recur.
>
> William Wimsatt, *The Prose Style of Samuel Johnson*, 12

Here the clause "that they recur" could become a noun: "The greatest obstacle to recognizing the expressive value of rhetorical devices is their recurrence." On the other hand, the phrase "the fact that" does have the effect of increasing the weight of the end of the sentence; perhaps "their frequent recurrence" would do the job.

> To be out in the street did not bring much relief either; the stench of the horses, the strong odors of the city intensified by the oppressive heat, was even more apparent the last days of summer. But what completely undermined my morale was the fact that I had no money. And with both Astruc and Weisweiler out of town I couldn't think of anybody to turn to for help. The small sum which I obtained at the Mont de Piété (the municipal pawnshop) for a suit and a coat

was good for a week with one frugal meal a day. And what a frustrating experience, this first visit to a pawnshop! When I arrived there, by Metro, the Mont de Piété was closed for the day, and I had to walk back, ashamed of being seen on the street with the two heavy garments on my arm. A cup of coffee and a roll was all I could afford to eat that day. I had to go through the same agony the next morning, but this time the place was open.

Arthur Rubinstein, My Young Years, Chapter 43

This passage is vivid and engaging, but the rhythm could be improved. The first sentence would have more impact if it ended with the strong sense impressions that Rubinstein mentions:

To be out in the street did not bring much relief either; the oppressive heat of these last days of summer intensified the stench of the horses and the strong odors of the city.

Then "the fact that" could be eliminated:

But what completely undermined my morale was my lack of money. And with both Astruc and Weisweiler out of town I couldn't think of anybody to turn to for help.

The rest of the passage needs to be rearranged. The frustrating first visit to the pawn shop should come first, before the small sum of money obtained on the second visit:

My first visit to the municipal pawnshop, the Mont de Piété—what a frustrating experience! When I arrived there, by Metro, the shop was closed for the day and I had to walk back, ashamed of being seen on the street with my suit and coat on my arm. A cup of coffee and a roll was all I could afford to eat that day. I had to go through the same agony the next morning, but this time the place was open. The small sum I obtained was good for a week with one frugal meal a day.

The story seems more vivid when the rhythm of the narrative coincides with the rhythm of events. But of course there are few absolute rules. As always, the task of the artist is to pay attention and to choose.

Earlier in this chapter I argued against the choppy rhythm created by frequent parenthetical interruptions of natural grammatical units. But in the right situation this kind of rhythm can become a virtue of style:

> Merton Densher, who passed the best hours of each night at the office of his newspaper, had at times, during the day, to make up for it, a sense, or at least an appearance, of leisure, in accordance with which he was not infrequently to be met, in different parts of the town, at moments when men of business are hidden from the public eye.

> Henry James, *The Wings of the Dove*, Chapter 3

The strength of James's style, of his voice, of his personality, can make this rhythm convincing, at least for a while. But as the passage continues, I, at least, for my part, begin to fidget:

> More than once, during the present winter's end, he had deviated, toward three o'clock, or toward four, into Kensington Gardens, where he might for a while, on each occasion, have been observed to demean himself as a person with nothing to do.

Who is in control here, the artist or the style? As the passage continues, the question appears to be answered in favor of the artist:

> He made his way indeed, for the most part, with a certain directness, over to the north side; but once that ground was reached his behavior was noticeably wanting in point. He moved seemingly at random from alley to alley; he stopped for no reason and remained idly agaze; he sat down in a chair and then changed to a bench; after which he walked about again only to repeat both the vagueness and the vivacity. Distinctly, he was a man with either nothing at all to do or with ever so much to think about; and it was not to be denied that the impression he might often thus easily make had the effect

of causing the burden of proof, in certain directions, to rest on him.
It was a little the fault of his aspect, his personal marks, which made
it almost impossible to name his profession.

Here we begin with another series of short units:

> He made his way
> indeed,
> for the most part,
> with a certain directness,
> over to the north side;

But the sentence ends with a long unit that requires no break at all (though
a break after "reached" is possible):

> but once that ground was reached his behavior was noticeably want-
> ing in point.

Then four clauses in roughly parallel structure, with initial repetition of the
subject pronoun, varied in the fourth clause by an initial adverbial phrase:

> He moved seemingly at random from alley to alley;
> he stopped for no reason and remained idly agaze;
> he sat down in a chair and then changed to a bench;
> after which he walked about again only to repeat both the vague-
> ness and the vivacity.

There is no difficulty here following either the syntax or the action, which
is described chronologically, so that the order of the words mimics the order
of Densher's imagined movements. Both the action and the style reflect his
state of mind. But if the description of Densher's movements is easy to read,
the interpretation of his motives is more difficult, left in an unresolved
antithesis:

> Distinctly,
> he was a man with either nothing at all to do
> or with ever so much to think about;

I am not, however, entirely convinced by the end of the passage:

> and it was not to be denied
> that the impression he might often thus easily make
> had the effect of causing the burden of proof,
> in certain directions,
> to rest on him.
> It was a little the fault of his aspect,
> his personal marks,
> which made it almost impossible to name his profession.

Some of this seems to me to be filler: "it was not to be denied"—did anyone try to deny it? And what is the meaning of "in certain directions"? And is it really Densher's profession that is the important question here? If not, does it deserve its position at the end of the paragraph?

One may like this style or not like it. One may wonder if the difficulty simply of getting through the sentences is compensated by rewards on some other level. But these are questions of high criticism, beyond the scope of this book. One may charge James with many crimes, but not inattention.

ɤ

ORNATE STYLE

Ornate, mannered prose begins with Gorgias (c. 483 to 376 BCE) and, as we shall see, continues today. He was born in Leontini, a Greek city in Italy, but he visited Athens in 427 BCE as an ambassador. While he was in Athens he gave a number of public speeches, which became the talk of the town. Here is an example of the Gorgianic style, in a translation that attempts to reproduce in English the effect of the Greek original:

> Embellishment to a city is courage; to a body, beauty; to a soul, wisdom; to a deed, virtue; to discourse, truth. But the opposite of these is lack of embellishment. Now a man, woman, discourse, work, city, deed, if deserving of praise must be honored with praise, but if undeserving must be censured. For it is alike aberration and stultification to censure the commendable and to commend the censurable. It is the duty of the same individual both to proclaim justice wholly, and to declaim against injustice holily, to confute the detractors of Helen, a woman concerning whom the poets' praise has been universal and univocal; celebration of her name has been the commemoration of her fame. But I desire by rational reason to free the lady's reputation, by disclosing her detractors as prevaricators, and by revealing the truth to put an end to error. That in nature and in nurture the lady was the fairest flower of men and women is not unknown, not even to the few, for her maternity was of Leda, her paternity immortal by generation, but mortal by reputation, of Tyndareus and of Zeus, of whom the one was reputed in the being, the other was asserted in the affirming; the former, the greatest of humanity, the latter, the lordliest of divinity.

> Gorgias, "Praise of Helen," based on a translation by LaRue Van Hook

And this bombast goes on for some pages. In Greek the effect is even more remarkable, because rhymes are easier to find in an inflected language.

The principal features of the Gorgianic style are three rhetorical figures: rhyme ("homoioteleuton" in Greek), verbal contrasts ("antithesis"), and the construction of phrases of equal length ("parisosis" or "isocolon"). Graphic analysis shows how these features (and some others) work in the English translation:

Embellishment to a city is courage;
    to a body, beauty;
    to a. soul, wisdom;
    to a deed, virtue;
    to discourse, truth.
But the opposite of these is lack of embellishment.
Now a man, woman, discourse, work, city, deed,
if deserving of praise must be
    honored with praise, but
if undeserving must be
    censured.
For it is alike aberration and
      stultification
    to censure the commendable and
    to commend the censurable.
It is the duty of the same individual both
    to proclaim justice wholly, and
    to declaim against injustice holily,
    to confute the detractors of Helen,
a woman concerning whom the poets' praise has been
    universal and
    univocal;
celebration of her name has been the
commemoration of her fame.
But I desire by rational reason to free the lady's reputation,
by disclosing her detractors as
      prevaricators,
and by revealing the truth

to put an end to error.
That in nature and in
    nurture
the lady was the fairest flower of men and women
is not unknown,
not even to the few, for
    her maternity was of Leda,
    her paternity immortal by generation, but
        mortal by reputation,
of Tyndareus and
of Zeus, of whom
    the one was reputed in the being,
    the other was asserted in the affirming;
the former,
    the greatest of humanity,
the latter,
    the lordliest of divinity.

A fashion for this ornate style swept through Athens. Many writers fell under its influence, including Thucydides, Antiphon, and Isocrates. Plato, however, made fun of it in several of his dialogues.

The Gorgianic style is not likely to appeal to many modern readers. I don't like it much myself, though I do find it fascinating as a chapter in the history of literary fashion. And there has been more than one such chapter. The Renaissance English writer John Lyly, who lived from about 1554 to 1606, wrote in a somewhat similar style, which in its time was much admired. The following passage comes from the beginning of his romance *Euphues: The Anatomy of Wit*, published in 1578:

There dwelt in Athens a young gentleman of great patrimony, & of so comely a personage, that it was doubted whether he were more bound to Nature for the lineaments of his person, or to Fortune for the increase of his possessions. But Nature impatient of comparisons, and as it were disdaining a companion, or copartner in her working, added to this comeliness of his body such a sharp capacity of mind, that not only she proved Fortune counterfeit, but was half of that opinion that she herself was only current.[1] This young gallant, of more wit than wealth, and yet of more wealth than wisdom, seeing himself inferior to none in pleasant conceits, thought himself superior to all in honest conditions, insomuch that he deemed himself so apt to all things, that he gave himself almost to nothing, but practicing of those things commonly which are incident to these sharp wits, fine phrases, smooth quipping, merry taunting, using jesting without mean, & abusing mirth without measure.

John Lyly, Euphues: The Anatomy of Wit, 91

This ornate style is called Euphuism, from the name of the protagonist of Lyly's tale. Lyly was by no means the only English writer of Euphuistic prose; even Shakespeare at times shows the influence of this ornate style.[2]

Like the Gorgianic style, Euphuism is characterized by antithesis, homoioteleuton, and isocolon. But Lyly does not stop with the three Gorgianic figures. He also uses alliteration, which is easier in English than rhyme, and elaborate comparisons, often taken from the world of nature. The passage just quoted, for example, continues: "As therefore the sweetest rose hath his prickle, the finest velvet his brack,[3] the fairest flower his bran, so the sharpest wit hath his wanton will, and the holiest head his wicked way." And hardly a page later, we learn that Euphues has decided to move to Naples, "a place of more pleasure than profit, and yet of more profit than piety. . . .whereby it is evidently seen that the fleetest fish swalloweth the delicatest bait, that the highest soaring hawk traineth to the lure, and that the wittiest sconce is inveigled with the sudden view of alluring vanities."

Ornate style, language that calls attention to itself, has been often criticized. Prose should be transparent, according to one common view: not a thing in itself but a representation of something outside itself, either the world or the mind of the author—what counts is the thing signified, not the signifier. On this view, rhetoric is the enemy of truth and sincerity. "Whenever I hear the expression 'great prose' or 'fine prose,'" the critic James Sutherland says, "I am apt to suspect that it is something which I should not greatly care to read. . . . Prose, it is true, touches on poetry at one extreme, and on pure scientific communication at the other; but at its most characteristic it occupies a wide field of humane discourse and intelligent discussion. It is good prose when it allows the writer's meaning to come through with the least possible loss of significance and nuance, as a land-scape is seen through a clear window."[4]

I would question Sutherland on three points, one theoretical, one aesthetic, and one practical. First, he seems to assume that meaning simply exists, prior to language, and that the job of language is merely to represent that pre-existing meaning. Even if we grant, as I think we must, that meaning can occur without words, a little introspection should demonstrate that expression often helps to form meaning, and that the possibilities of expression influence the possibilities of meaning. Second, Sutherland seems to ignore the pleasure of self-conscious expression, or at least it tends to limit that pleasure to something called poetry. But why should poets have all the fun? Third, he fails to account for the continuing popularity of ornate prose.

Ornamentation in itself is not inherently bad. The problem with Lyly's style, for example, is not ornament but monotony. It would be unfair to call him a one-trick pony, but he uses the same half-dozen gimmicks over and over again, throughout the tale; 60 pages of alliteration and antithesis are more than enough. Yet ornate style is not to be scorned just because of one bad example. If all prose were pedestrian, the world would be a poor place indeed.

Dickens, for example, often opened a novel with a rhetorical flourish, based on a single figure. He did not sustain the figure past the first few paragraphs, however, and he used different figures for different books. *A Tale of Two Cities* begins with a series of antitheses, to produce an extended paradox:

> It was the best of times, it was the worst of times, it was the age of wisdom, it was the age of foolishness, it was the epoch of belief, it was the epoch of incredulity, it was the season of Light, it was the season of Darkness, it was the spring of hope, it was the winter of despair, we had everything before us, we had nothing before us, we were all going direct to Heaven, we were all going direct the other way—in short, the period was so far like the present period, that some of its noisiest authorities insisted on its being received, for good or for evil, in the superlative degree of comparison only.

Charles Dickens, *A Tale of Two Cities*, Chapter 1

Hard Times begins with insistent repetition of the word "Facts":

> "Now, what I want is Facts. Teach these boys and girls nothing but
> Facts. Facts alone are wanted in life. Plant nothing else, and root out
> everything else. You can only form the minds of reasoning animals
> upon Facts: nothing else will ever be of any service to them. This is
> the principle on which I bring up my own children, and this is the
> principle on which I bring up these children. Stick to the Facts, sir!"
>
> Charles Dickens, *Hard Times,* Chapter 1

And *Bleak House* begins with a series of sentence fragments describing the
dreary November weather:

> London. Michaelmas term lately over, and the Lord Chancellor sit-
> ting in Lincoln's Inn Hall. Implacable November weather. As much
> mud in the streets, as if the waters had but newly retired from the
> face of the earth, and it would not be wonderful to meet a
> Megalosaurus, forty feet long or so, waddling like an elephantine
> lizard up Holborn Hill. Smoke lowering down from chimney-pots,
> making a soft black drizzle, with flakes of soot in it as big as full-
> grown snow-flakes—gone into mourning, one might imagine, for
> the death of the sun. Dogs, undistinguishable in mire. Horses, scarce-
> ly better; splashed to their very blinkers. Foot passengers, jostling one
> another's umbrellas, in a general infection of ill-temper, and losing
> their foot-hold at street-corners, where tens of thousands of other
> foot passengers have been slipping and sliding since the day broke (if
> this day ever broke), adding new deposits to the crust upon crust of
> mud, sticking at those points tenaciously to the pavement, and accu-
> mulating at compound interest.
>
> Charles Dickens, *Bleak House*, Chapter 1

Dickens favored a particular kind of ornate style, an incantatory elo-
quence, for death scenes, particularly when they involved children. The
following passages, from the beginning and end of a chapter titled "What
The Waves Were Always Saying," describe the sad death of young Paul
Dombey:

Paul had never risen from his little bed. He lay there, listening to the voices in the street, quite tranquilly; not caring much how the time went, but watching it and watching everything about him with observing eyes.

When the sunbeams struck into his room through the rustling blinds, and quivered on the opposite wall like golden water, he knew that evening was coming on, and that the sky was red and beautiful. As the reflection died away, and a gloom went creeping up the wall, he watched it deepen, deepen, deepen, into night. Then he thought how the long streets were dotted with lamps, and how the peaceful stars were shining overhead. His fancy had a strange tendency to wander to the river, which he knew was flowing through the great city; and now he thought how black it was, and how deep it would look, reflecting the hosts of stars—and more than all, how steadily it rolled away to meet the sea.

. . .

The golden ripple on the wall came back again, and nothing else stirred in the room. The old, old Fashion! The fashion that came in with our first garments, and will last unchanged until our race has run its course, and the wide firmament is rolled up like a scroll. The old, old fashion—Death!

Oh thank God, all who see it, for that older fashion yet, of Immortality! And look upon us, angels of young children, with regards not quite estranged, when the swift river bears us to the ocean.

Charles Dickens, *Dombey and Son*, 207 and 212

"Poetic" styles of this kind—sonorous, repetitive, florid, imagistic—remain quite popular even in our own time, as we will see in a moment. I am not sure, however, that it is quite right to call them poetic: certainly there is nothing that we could call a "poetic" style of poetry. Is the style of Pope the style of Blake? Is the style of Frost the style of Ginsberg? On the contrary, a passage like the death of Paul Dombey is not poetic but rhetorical—just as rhetorical as the style of Gorgias or Lyly—even if some of the tricks are different. For example, immediate repetitions such as "deepen, deepen, deepen" (the technical term is *epizeuxis*) are rare in Gorgias or Lyly.

And even when the tricks are the same, they are used for different purposes. In the description of Paul Dombey's death there is an antithesis, but only one: Paul lay in bed (a) "not caring much how the time went,"(b) "but watching it and watching everything about him with observing eyes." Because there is only the one antithesis, our attention is not brought to it as a figure in itself, as a form of language; whereas Lyly forces us, through repetition, to notice the figure as a figure, Dickens merely uses it to say something about Paul's state of mind. Still, it would be wrong to suggest that Dickens' language is transparent, like a clear glass window; he wanted his language to be noticed, or at least felt.

Any listing of the rhetorical figures used in a passage tends to isolate devices that really work together. Words are chosen not just for meaning but also for sound. They are ordered to produce a particular rhythm; meaning, sound, and rhythm join to form the pattern of images. Moreover, the topic—death—will predispose the reader to respond to these devices with the appropriate emotion. Thus "the sunbeams struck into his room through the rustling blinds, and quivered on the opposite wall like golden water"; but in the evening, "a gloom went creeping up the wall." The sounds and the rhythms of the words work with the meanings to create an effect of tranquil pathos. But death is not always tragic, at least in literature, and a different set of devices could induce a different feeling.

Rhetorical prose continued to be popular through the twentieth century. A few excerpts will demonstrate some typical devices. I begin with a passage from T.E. Lawrence's *Seven Pillars of Wisdom*—a remarkable book, though one that requires some patience from the reader. Here is the first paragraph:

Some of the evil of my tale may have been inherent in our circumstances. For years we lived anyhow with one another in the naked desert, under the indifferent heaven. By day the hot sun fermented us; and we were dizzied by the beating wind. At night we were stained by dew, and shamed into pettiness by the innumerable silences of stars. We were a self-centered army without parade or gesture, devoted to freedom, the second of man's creeds, a purpose so ravenous that it devoured all our strength, a hope so transcendent that our earlier ambitions faded in its glare.

T.E. Lawrence, *Seven Pillars of Wisdom*, 27

Here, as in the passage from Dickens, the words are chosen for rhetorical effect. "Evil," of course, is about as strong a word as there is in the language; its effect is heightened by the adjectives "naked" and "indifferent" and by the verbs "fermented" and "dizzied." The phrase "the innumerable silences of stars" has rhythm, alliteration, and a transferred epithet (it is, after all, the stars that are innumerable) that multiplies astronomically the silences of space and the desert. There is no epizeuxis in this passage, but a little later on the same page we find that God was "merciless, merciless."

Another feature of this kind of prose is the accumulation of elements at the end of a sentence. At the end of the present passage Lawrence describes his companions as "a self-centered army" "without parade or gesture," "devoted to freedom." Freedom, in turn, is "the second of man's creeds"; it is both "a purpose so ravenous that it devoured all our strength" and "a hope so transcendent that our earlier ambitions faded in its glare." All these phrases are tacked on to the end of the sentence, in a variety of grammatical constructions: an adjectival prepositional phrase, an adjectival participial phrase, and two appositives.

The following passage is another example of the accumulating style, and here the grammar is at times quite loose:

> Sometimes one meets a woman who is beast turning to human. Such a person's every movement will reduce to an image of a forgotten experience: a mirage of an eternal wedding cast on the racial memory; as insupportable a joy as would be the vision of an eland coming down an aisle of trees, chapleted with orange blossoms and bridal veil, a hoof raised in the economy of fear, stepping in the trepidation of flesh that will become myth; as the unicorn is neither man nor beast deprived, but human hunger pressing its breast to its prey.
>
> Djuna Barnes, *Nightwood*, 37

A long sentence in this style is like a journey along an obscured path: the eyes cannot see or the mind anticipate the inevitable goal. The beast woman's movement reduces to an image of a forgotten experience, and this image is a mirage of an eternal wedding. Then something—either the mirage or the wedding—is as insupportable a joy as the vision of an eland; this eland would be coming down an aisle of trees; it would be chapleted with orange blossoms and bridal veil. Now both the grammar and the meaning become vague: "a hoof raised in the economy of fear" seems loosely connected to the grammar of the sentence as a whole (in what is called an absolute construction), and "the economy of fear" sounds impressive, but I'm not sure that "economy" means very much. The participle "stepping," which must modify "an eland," returns to the grammar of the sentence. But the ending of the sentence is again only loosely connected to the grammar of the sentence: although the conjunction "as" can be quite precise if the ideas it links are clearly related, it can also be quite indefinite if the relationship is left unspecified. I do not mean these comments to sound negative. I find this passage, particularly the ending, quite effective; but part of the effect is achieved through a rhetoric of blurred grammar and indistinct meaning.

Seven Pillars of Wisdom was written in 1919, though not published for some years; *Nightwood* was published in 1936. Further examples would be easy to find. Virginia Woolf, William Faulkner, and William Gaddis are only three of the many well-known twentieth century writers who have used the figures of rhetoric to produce so-called poetic prose. Of course their individual styles vary widely, but they are all ornate, and they are all rhetorical. Here is an ornate passage from John Hawkes' *Second Skin*, which was published in the mid-1960s. In it the first-person narrator, a former naval officer known as the Skipper, has been convinced by his daughter Cassandra to get a tattoo. The other characters mentioned are Sonny, the Skipper's faithful servant, and Tremlow, who raped the Skipper during a mutiny:

> The scream—yes, I confess it, scream—that was clamped between my teeth was a strenuous black bat struggling, wrestling in my bloated mouth and with every puncture of the needle—fast as the stinging of artificial bees, this exquisite torture—I with my eyes squeezed tight, my lips squeezed tight, felt that at any moment it must thrust the slimy black tip of its archaic skeletal wing out into view of Cassandra and the working tattooer. But I was holding on. I longed to disgorge the bat, to sob, to be flung into the relief of freezing water like an old woman submerged and screaming in the wild balm of some dark baptismal rite in a roaring river. But I was holding on. While the punctures were marching across, burning

their open pinprick way across my chest, I was bulging in every muscle, slick, strained, and the bat was peering into my mouth of pain, kicking, slick with my saliva, and in the stuffed interior of my brain I was resisting, jerking in outraged helplessness, blind and baffled, sick with the sudden recall of what Tremlow had done to me that night—helpless abomination—while Sonny lay sprawled on the bridge and the captain trembled on his cot behind the pilothouse. There were tiny fat glistening tears in the corners of my eyes. But they never fell. Never from the eyes of this heavy bald-headed once-handsome man. Victim. Courageous victim.

John Hawkes, *Second Skin*, 19

The style is highly rhetorical, relying on many of the figures used in previous examples: alliteration, repetition, dramatic rhythm, violent imagery, a profusion of adjectives, and a loose accumulation of grammatical structure. Such a style cries out to be declaimed, to be intoned, to be acted. Can we take such writing seriously?[5] Did Hawkes want us to take it seriously? Perhaps the excess is deliberate parody. Serious or not, the effect depends on devices used with entire solemnity by other writers. Parody, especially, must refer to something real.

The so-called poetic style is not the only ornate style of our time. The following passage is insistently self-conscious and ornate, but it is not poetic—at least not in the way the passages above are poetic:

Personally of course I regret everything. Not a word, not a deed, not a thought, not a need, not a grief, not a joy, not a girl, not a boy, not a doubt, nor a trust, not a scorn, not a lust, not a hope, not a fear, not a smile, not a tear, not a name, not a face, no time, no place, that I do not regret, exceedingly. An ordure, from beginning to end. And yet, when I sat for Fellowship, but for the boil on my bottom. . . The rest, an ordure. The Tuesday scowls, the Wednesday growls, the Thursday curses, the Friday howls, the Saturday snores, the Sunday yawns, the Monday morns, the Monday morns. The whacks, the moans, the cracks, the groans, the welts, the squeaks, the belts, the shrieks, the pricks, the prayers, the kicks, the tears, the skelps, and the yelps.

Samuel Beckett, *Watt*, 46

Beckett does not persist in this style for very long, but much of the novel is just as ornate in one way or another. Like Lyly, Beckett picks a rhetorical device and works it for all it's worth, though his repertoire is more varied. His rhythmic units are often short and abrupt, even in long sentences. *Watt* is not an easy read, though it can be very entertaining; other of Beckett's works, such as *How It Is*, are even more extreme. At times he seems to resist the notion that language ought to mean something.

The passages I have selected for this chapter might seem to prove, as C.S. Baldwin says, that, "The style inevitably acquired by those who seek style is decorative and elaborate." There is, however, another manner of writing, equally rhetorical but severe and curt rather than decorative and elaborate. This style is sometimes called Senecan, after Lucius Annaeus Seneca, a Latin writer of the first century CE; but it also had other ancient sources, in particular Cornelius Tacitus (late first and early second centuries), and Gaius Sallustius Crispus (first century BCE), known in English as Sallust. The Senecan style was important in the sixteenth and seventeenth centuries, partly as a reaction to the long, complex sentences of the Ciceronian style, which I will discuss in a later chapter. In the twentieth century, perhaps the most conscious imitator of the Senecan style was Ronald Syme, a Roman historian who happened to be an authority on Sallust. Syme favored short sentences—even sentence fragments—and most of his longer sentences are formed with coordinating conjunctions; subordinate clauses are very rare in his work:

> The fashion persists of condemning and deploring the last epoch of the Roman Republic. It was turbulent, corrupt, immoral. And some speak of decadence. On the contrary, it was an era of liberty, vitality —and innovation.
>
> . . .
>
> This liberal and humane evolution is seldom appraised as it deserves. Sallust himself is partly to blame. Not that he wasted words or regrets on the decay of religion. But he wrote in revulsion from his own time. He interpreted a process of economic change and political adjustment in terms of morals; and he fell an easy prey to conventional notions about old Roman virtue.
>
> Ronald Syme, *Sallust*, 16

This style is the opposite of ornate, but it is no less self-conscious and rhetorical.

In twentieth-century fiction the most noted curt stylist is Ernest Hemingway; here is a passage from *A Farewell to Arms*:

> We drank the second grappa, Rinaldi put away the bottle and we went down the stairs. It was hot walking through the town but the sun was starting to go down and it was very pleasant. The British hospital was a big villa build by Germans before the war. Miss Barkley was in the garden. Another nurse was with her. We saw their white uniforms through the trees and walked towards them. Rinaldi saluted. I saluted too but more moderately.
>
> Ernest Hemingway, *A Farewell to Arms*, 17–18

Hemingway is often considered an anti-rhetorical writer. Far from it. He merely uses a different kind of rhetoric.

5

A FEW FIGURES OF SPEECH

In the previous chapter I focused on the ornate style in a few of its manifestations and discussed some of the figures of speech used in such writing. In this chapter I want to look at a few more figures and how they are used in a variety of styles.[1] Something over two hundred figures of speech have been named, and others occur that remain nameless. Most of the names are Greek or Latin, and although a few (like "metaphor" or "climax") have become naturalized in English, others, such as "hendiadys," sound foreign and intimidating. To the Greeks and Romans who coined them, these terms made perfect sense. For instance, *hendiadys* comes from a Greek phrase meaning "one [thing] through two [things]" and designates a figure in which a noun-plus-adjective combination is made into two nouns: a standard example is "by length of time and siege" instead of "by a long siege." Some rhetoricians have attempted to find English equivalents for all the classic rhetorical terms; the best example is George Puttenham, whose book *The Arte of English Poesie* was published in 1589; he called hendiadys "twinnes." But the English terms have never taken hold, so unless there is an adequate English equivalent I will use the standard Greek and Latin.

Of the roughly two hundred named figures of speech, probably only twenty-five or thirty are useful for most writers to have in ready memory; the others can stay in the textbooks for reference when needed. I will pass over, for example, *accusatio concertativa*, also called *anticategoria*, which means "mutual accusation or recrimination" and is likely more applicable to divorce courts or political campaigns than to literature. I will also pass over *anemographia*, "a description of the wind," which is a little too specialized for most purposes.

Because rhetoric was first developed by Greek and Latin writers, some of its figures are more appropriate in those inflected languages than they are in English. In *polyptoton*, for instance, a single word is used in different grammatical forms. In following lines from Catullus, the relative pronoun appears in the forms "qui" (in the combined form "quicum"), "quem," and "cui" (which Catullus may have spelled "quoi"); since these are in emphatic positions, it seems likely that Catullus wanted the variation to be noticeable:

> Passer, deliciae meae puellae,
> *qui*cum ludere, *quem* in sinu tenere,
> *cui* primum digitum dare appententi
> et acris solet incitare morsus . . .

> Sparrow, my girl's darling,
> *Whom* she plays with, *whom* she cuddles,
> *Whom* she likes to tempt with finger-
> Tip and teases to nip harder . . .

Translation by Guy Lee, The Poems of Catullus, 3

Lee's translation keeps the emphatic position of the relative pronouns, but in English they all have the same form, so the polyptoton is lost. A more literal (and much less poetic) translation might be *"with whom* she is accustomed to play, *whom* she is accustomed to cuddle, *to whom* she is accustomed to give her fingertip. . . ."[3]

As my quasi-literal translation suggests, English often uses prepositions to express what Latin and Greek express through the inflection of cases; Abraham Lincoln's famous phrase "government of the people, by the people, and for the people" is a sort of polyptoton through prepositions. But this figure is rare in English.

A different kind of polyptoton, however, is not uncommon. In this figure a single semantic root appears in different parts of speech. So, for example, in Vladimir Nabokov's *Ada*[4] we find "a specular, and hence speculatory, phenomenon" (19); "all the divinities and divines" (21); "revived the part while vivifying the whole" (31); "the collected works of unrecollected authors" (41); and so on.

Over the centuries various attempts have been made to categorize the figures of speech. No system has achieved general acceptance, but one common classification distinguishes between *tropes*, in which the usual meaning of a word is changed or extended, and *schemes*, in which the meaning is left alone; most schemes involve the ordering or repetition of words or sounds. This distinction has a certain use, but it quickly breaks down, since almost any figure can be called upon to change the meaning of words in some way—rhyme, for example, often tends to suggest some otherwise unsuspected semantic connection between the rhyming words, in addition to their similarity in sound. But some figures seem to involve meaning more readily than others: metaphor is essentially a trope, whereas rhyme is primarily a scheme, even though it can affect the way a word is understood. Perhaps the distinction should apply to the use of the figure rather than to the figure itself. In any case, modern literary criticism has concentrated on tropes, particularly metaphor and other types of symbolism.[5] In this chapter I will be concerned mostly with schemes.

Alliteration: Some figures are simply figures of sound. Of these the best known and most commonly used is *alliteration*: the repetition of initial sounds, usually initial consonant sounds.[6] (Other figures of sound are *assonance*, the repetition of vowel sounds; *parechesis*, the repetition of the same sounds in words in close succession; and *parimion*, alliteration in which every word in a phrase or a sentence begins with the same letter.) Alliteration can produce quite a variety of effects, but it almost always creates some sort of emphasis. This figure is often found in passages of "poetic" description:

> She pushes a tendril of hair behind her ear, a strand that has escaped the braid. This strand contains some threads of grey. She stares at the envelope, then lifts her head to watch the departure of the mail sled, its driver and team of noisy dogs, to watch it glide over the snow-covered ice and disappear behind Burnt Island. For several minutes she wants to refuse the message she has not yet read. The world around her is quiet and fixed, frozen and beautiful. She does not want the scene disturbed. Even the tracks of the sled irritate her; they have scarred the white surface, they have soiled the day.
>
> Jane Urquhart, *The Underpainter*, 4

The strongest alliteration here comes in the last sentence, with the words *sled*, *scarred*, *surface*, and *soiled*, but sibilants are repeated throughout. Also worth noting is the emphasis achieved through the accented single syllables of "not yet read," as well as the parallelism in the phrase "quiet and fixed, frozen and beautiful," with the alliteration of "fixed" and "frozen," and the longest word at the end.

In the next passage the second sentence is almost entirely alliterative, and the alliteration is reinforced by the rhythm, which seems reminiscent of a nursery rhyme:

> Outside staircases were everywhere. Winding ones, wooden ones, rusty and risky ones. An endless repetition of precious peeling balconies and waste lots making the occasional gap here and there.
>
> Mordecai Richler, The Street, 23

In the third sentence the alliteration of "precious" and "peeling" creates the expectation of more, but this expectation is disappointed. The following passage also creates an expectation:

> Dickens said savagely that his world was an inferno of intolerance, a privy of pride, a graveyard of greed, a sewer of selfishness, a pit of privilege, a dungeon of caste, a wasteland of filth, a rat-warren of lawyers, a paradox of preachers, an abscission of teachers, and a parliament of fools.
>
> Earle Davis, The Flint and the Flame: The Artistry of
Charles Dickens, 310

The four alliterated pairs —privy/pride, graveyard/greed, sewer/selfishness, pit/privilege—are certainly impressive, especially since they are introduced by the alliterated "said savagely," but when the pattern fails, the reader may feel that a promise has been broken; "a paradox of preachers" is hardly sufficient compensation. (I don't count "inferno" and "intolerance," since the accented syllables are not alliterated.) Putting all the alliterated pairs at the end would eliminate the problem of disappointed expectation:

> Dickens said savagely that his world was an inferno of intolerance, a dungeon of caste, a wasteland of filth, a rat-warren of lawyers, an abscission of teachers, a parliament of fools, a privy of pride, a graveyard of greed, a sewer of selfishness, a pit of privilege, and a paradox of preachers.

But the passage could still use more work. "Abscission," which means "a cutting off," is weak compared to the concrete and vivid "privy," "grave-yard," "sewer," and so on. And perhaps "parliament of fools" made a more satisfying end after all. Perhaps there is some extrinsic reason for the order of the list. Did Davis take all these phrases from Dickens himself (perhaps in chronological order)? If so, they might remain unchanged. If not, it might be possible to find other words to make all the pairs alliterate; but then the result might be excessive.

Alliteration seems to invite excess:

> I put it to you, sir, that Lucian needs not to say another word, but we know that Demonax had loved letters, and partly by aid of them had arrived at being such a man. No; by consent of all, literature is a nurse of noble natures, and right reading makes a full man in a sense even better than Bacon's; not replete, but complete rather, to the pattern for which Heaven designed him.

> Sir Arthur Quiller-Couch, *The Art of Writing*, 7

Used in moderation, to call attention to particular words, alliteration can be quite effective. In the next passage the young Prince Rasselas is travel-ling the world in search of wisdom; having admired the philosophic decla-mation of a public orator, he pays this sage a private visit, and finds him in despair over the death of his daughter. The alliteration at the end of the pas-sage ironically illustrates the point of the episode:

> "Have you forgotten the precepts," said Rasselas, "which you so powerfully enforce? Has wisdom no strength to arm the heart against calamity? Consider that external things are naturally variable, but truth and reason are always the same." "What comfort," said the mourner, "can truth and reason afford me? Of what effect are they now, but to tell me that my daughter will not be restored?"
>
> The prince, whose humanity would not suffer him to insult misery with reproof, went away convinced of the emptiness of rhetorical sound, and the inefficacy of polished periods and studied sentences.

> Samuel Johnson, *Rasselas*, Chapter 18

Alliteration is often combined with other figures of sound or rhythm. In the following passage alliteration emphasizes three antitheses:

> Nature, culture, gender, myth, East, West, truth—the degree to which these concepts are not transcendent universals but are socially constructed has finally hit us. Cultural anthropology will mold the shape of classical studies for this generation. This is an exciting but also difficult situation: to be fully and honestly philologists, we must now learn our Geertz along with Greek, absorb Lienhardt as well as Latin, undertake ethnography after epigraphy.

> Richard Martin, "The Seven Sages as Performers of Wisdom," 108

These pairs work well; Greek, Latin, and epigraphy are three essential tools of traditional philology; Clifford Geertz and Godfrey Lienhardt are important ethnographers, who represent exactly the kind of new scholarship Martin demands. The effect does not seem farfetched. And here we find an essential principle of rhetoric: readers should never have cause to feel that the figure has been purchased at the expense of the meaning—unless, of course, the figure is the point of the passage.

Asyndeton and Polysyndeton: Most rhetorical schemes concern words, their addition, subtraction, repetition, or arrangement. One of the simplest of these is *asyndeton*, in which conjunctions are left out. In the following passage we would expect the conjunction "and" to precede the final word of the last sentence, "Shakespeare":

> In England and Spain there was scarcely any classicizing drama which was successful. But the English and Spanish dramatists assimilated much of the classical drama, and added their own imagination to it; reshaped its characters, its humor, and its conventions to suit their peoples, and left the rest. The magnificent result was Marlowe, Lope de Vega, Webster, Calderon, Shakespeare.

> Gilbert Highet, *The Classical Tradition*, 129

Many rhetorical figures can be found even in rather popular writing; here is an example of asyndeton in a series of infinitive phrases from

Interview with the Vampire, a novel best known for qualities other than the elegance of its style:

> It took a moment for the boy to wipe his forehead and his lips with a handkerchief, to stammer that the microphone was in the machine, to press the button, to say that the machine was on.
>
> Anne Rice, *Interview with the Vampire*, 3

This example notwithstanding, asyndeton is more frequent in ornate prose; the following excerpt offers several instances in the space of a single paragraph. Some background is necessary for this passage and the one following. The hero of Salman Rushdie's *Shame*, Omar Khayyam Shakil, is the child of three sisters; when one of the sisters becomes pregnant by an unknown father, the three women decide to participate equally in mothering the child. All three show the signs of pregnancy, all undergo labor, all nurse the infant. They live as recluses in a huge and decaying mansion full of innumerable antiques and treasures. Omar first sees the outside world at the age of ten, when he comes across a broken wall in a room that he is never able to find again. When he is twelve he finds a telescope, with which he spies on the people of the town, and especially on a young girl, Farah Zoroaster. He then persuades his mothers to let him leave the house to go to school in the town. In this passage he is telling Farah about his house:

> "Sometimes I found skeletons," he swore to disbelieving Farah, "human as well as animal." And even where bones were absent, the house's long-dead occupants dogged his steps. Not in the way you think!—no howls, no clanking chains!—But disembodied feelings, the choking fumes of ancient hopes, fears, loves; and finally, made wild by the ancestor-heavy, phantom oppressions of these far recesses of the run-down building, Omar Khayyam took his revenge (not long after the episode of the broken wall) on his unnatural surroundings. I wince as I record his vandalism: armed with broomstick and misappropriated hatchet, he rampaged through dusty passages and maggoty bedrooms, smashing glass cabinets, felling oblivion-sprinkled divans, pulverizing wormy libraries; crystal, paintings, rusty helmets,

the paper-thin remnants of priceless silken carpets were destroyed
beyond all possibility of repair.

Salman Rushdie, *Shame*, 27

It is easy to pass over asyndeton; on first reading I noticed only one example in this passage, and it was not till I went back over it that I found the
others. The first is the phrase "no howls, no clanking chains!"; next is
"hopes, fears, loves." The third is a series of participial phrases: "smashing
glass cabinets, felling oblivion-sprinkled divans, pulverizing wormy
libraries"; and the fourth is a series of subjects "crystal, paintings, rusty hel-
mets, the paper-thin remnants of priceless silken carpets were destroyed
beyond all possibility of repair."

Polysyndeton is the use of more conjunctions than necessary. Again Rushdie
provides an illustration; here he is describing the triple birth of his hero:

When Hashmat Bibi heard a key turning in the door and came
timidly into the room with food and drink and fresh sheets and
sponges and soap and towels, she found the three sisters sitting up
together in the capacious bed, the same bed in which their father
had died, a huge mahogany four-poster around whose columns
carved serpents coiled upwards to the brocade Eden of the canopy.
They were all wearing the flushed expression of dilated joy that is
the mother's true prerogative; and the baby was passed from breast
to breast, and none of the six was dry.

Salman Rushdie, *Shame*, 14

Here too the same figure is used more than once—first in a series of
nouns ("food and drink and fresh sheets and sponges and soap and towels"),
then in a series of clauses ("They were all wearing the flushed expression
of dilated joy that is the mother's true prerogative; and the baby was passed
from breast to breast, and none of the six was dry.")

Sometimes asyndeton and polysyndeton can be combined in a single
passage:

The woman's winters are long and bright and silent. Just before nightfall the landscape blossoms into various shades of blue. Few events interrupt the tranquillity; a storm, maybe, or the delivery of supplies, or her own infrequent journeys over ice, around Thunder Cape, into Port Arthur. She has come to rely on the predictability of the season, its lengthiness, its cold. She doubts she would be able to understand a life without it.

Jane Urquhart, *The Underpainter*, 4

Asyndeton and polysyndeton are simple figures, easy to spot, easy to describe, easy to create. But they are not easy to interpret. Why would a writer want to use asyndeton or polysyndeton in any particular instance? What is the effect of either figure? Is the effect always the same? Sometimes asyndeton seems to give a sense that the list could be extended at will, as in the first example cited: Marlowe, Lope de Vega, Webster, Calderon, Shakespeare. And sometimes polysyndeton seems to give a sense of exhausting all relevant possibilities, as in "food and drink and fresh sheets and sponges and soap and towels." But I am not sure that every use of these figures can be accounted for so simply. "The woman's winters are long and bright and silent"—is there the sense that a list has been exhausted? Or is there just a lingering over the sounds of the words? "She has come to rely on the predictability of the season, its lengthiness, its cold"—is there the sense that a list could be extended at will? What happens if the one figure is turned into the other? "When Hashmat Bibi heard a key turning in the door and came timidly into the room with food, drink, fresh sheets, sponges, soap, towels"—if this had been printed, would we know that it was not what the writer intended?

In general, it is easier to name a figure than to explain its effect. Perhaps there are no words in the language to designate the subtle nuances created by these figures. In any case, a name would not be an explanation. The writer probably relies on feeling the passage, feeling the rhythm and the emphasis, without much in the way of conscious explanation or justification. And probably the reader does the same in reverse, working from the words on the page to the feeling they somehow express.

Anaphora: Another simple figure is *anaphora*, the repetition of a word at the

beginning of successive clauses or sentences. The figure is particularly satisfying if the repeated word is the important word in its clause. The following passage is a discussion of procrastinating characters in several of Henry
James's later novels: Strether in *The Ambassadors*, Densher and Milly in *The
Wings of the Dove*, and Maggie in *The Golden Bowl*:

> But Strether procrastinates in a deeper sense as well: for as long as he
> is able, he avoids any conscious knowledge of the affair between
> Chad and Madame de Vionnet. To face that knowledge is for
> Strether far more terrible than to face the awe-inspiring Mrs.
> Newsome. Postponing conscious recognition, he remains—at least
> temporarily—safe: safe as Densher is, anxiously suppressing full
> awareness of the plot against Milly; safe as Milly herself, struggling
> to avoid the certain knowledge of her own death; safe even as
> Maggie at the beginning of *The Golden Bowl*, unconsciously pro-
> longing her dream of innocence.

> Ruth Bernard Yeazell, *Language and Knowledge in the
> Late Novels of Henry James*, 21-2

Not only does Yeazell use anaphora here, but she repeats the word "safe" at
the end of one clause and the beginning of another: "he remains . . . safe:
safe as Densher is." This figure is called "anadiplosis" or "anastrophe."

In the following example, the predicate adjective "beautiful" is repeated
twice in anaphora. Here Norman Mailer is describing the astronaut Neil
Armstrong's recurrent childhood dream:

> It was a beautiful dream—to hold one's breath and to levitate; not
> to fly and not to fall, but to hover. It was beautiful because it might
> soon prove to be prophetic, beautiful because it was profound and it
> was mysterious, beautiful because it was appropriate to a man who
> would land on the moon.

> Norman Mailer, *Of a Fire on the Moon*, 45

As this passage shows, anaphora can include more than one word. Here
is another example of anaphora with two words:

The sisters sat silent, waiting for the wedding party to come out. Gudrun was impatient of talk. She wanted to think about Gerald Crich. She wanted to see if the strong feeling she had got from him was real. She wanted to have herself ready.

   Inside the church, the wedding was going on. Hermione Roddice was thinking only of Birkin. He stood near her. She seemed to gravitate physically towards him. She wanted to stand touching him. She could hardly be sure he was near her, if she did not touch him. Yet she stood subjected through the wedding service.

D.H. Lawrence, Women in Love, 23

In the first paragraph the anaphora consists of the words "She wanted" plus an infinitive phrase, repeated three times. In the second paragraph the anaphora is reduced to the single word "She," although in one instance it is followed by the same structure used in the first paragraph, "wanted" plus an infinitive. The use of anaphora in these two paragraphs sets up a parallel between Gudrun and Hermione that echoes a larger parallel, between Gudrun and her sister Ursula, which runs through the whole novel.

   In addition to anaphora of words, there can be anaphora of grammatical constructions. In the following passage only the subject pronoun "they" is repeated, but it is regularly followed by the verb:

He [the emperor Probus] vanquished the Burgundians, a considerable people of the Vandalic race. They had wandered in quest of booty from the banks of the Oder to those of the Seine. They esteemed themselves sufficiently fortunate to purchase, by the restitution of their booty, the permission of an undisturbed retreat. They attempted to elude that article of the treaty. Their punishment was immediate and terrible.

   Edward Gibbon, *The Decline and Fall of the Roman Empire*, Chapter 12

The series "They had wandered/They esteemed/They attempted" emphasizes the verbs and makes the variation of construction in the last sentence—"Their punishment was immediate"—all the more emphatic. It's worth noting that Lawrence, in the second of the two paragraphs quoted above, follows a similar pattern: "She seemed to gravitate" / "She wanted to stand" / "She could hardly be sure" / "Yet she stood." I think, though, that the Gibbon example is the more successful. By varying the construction of the verb in the third sentence—"She could hardly be"—Lawrence weakens the effect of the repetition.

As a rule, anaphora is used only sparingly; variation in sentence structure is more highly valued. But some writers create their styles precisely by violating the rules:

> Melanctha Herbert had not made her life all simple like Rose Johnson. Melanctha had not found it easy with herself to make her wants and what she had, agree.
>
> Melanctha Herbert was always losing what she had in wanting all the things she saw. Melanctha was always being left when she was not leaving others.
>
> Melanctha Herbert always loved too hard and much too often.
>
> Gertrude Stein, "Melanctha," in *Three Lives*, 89

Another five paragraphs follow, each beginning "Melanctha"; then after a one-paragraph break, four more paragraphs begin the same way. Similar constructions recur throughout the story.

Epistrophe or Antistrophe: A repeated word at the end of a series of sentences is called *epistrophe* or *antistrophe*:

> All roads lead to Johannesburg. If you are white or if you are black they lead to Johannesburg. If the crops fail, there is work in Johannesburg. If there are taxes to be paid, there is work in Johannesburg. If the farm is too small to be divided further, some must go to Johannesburg. If there is a child to be born that must be delivered in secret, it can be delivered in Johannesburg.
>
> Alan Paton, *Cry, the Beloved Country*, 52

The epistrophe in the next passage is less effective:

> In the light of this theory it becomes evident, first, that Shakespeare's development of his subject matter and his mode of expression in his

plays and poems are characteristic of his time; secondly, that he utilized every resource of thought and language known to his time;
thirdly, that his genius, outrunning precept even while conforming
to it, transcends that of his contemporaries and belongs to all time.

Sister Miriam Joseph, *Rhetoric in Shakespeare's Time*, 4

In the first two clauses the emphasis must fall on "characteristic" and
"known," and "time" feels like an anticlimax. In the third clause the last two
words can each take stress, but "all" is probably the more emphatic. A sim-
pler version might be better:

In the light of this theory it becomes evident that Shakespeare, in
the development of his subject matter and his mode of expression,
used every resource of thought and language known to and characteristic of his time; but his transcendent genius, outrunning precept
even while conforming to it, belongs to all time.

The point of the passage is that Shakespeare both typifies his time and transcends it; two clauses, then, are needed, not three, especially since there is not
much difference between the idea that "his mode of expression" is "characteristic of his time" and the idea that "he utilized every resource of thought
and language known to his time." But I am not satisfied with this version
either. Perhaps the style is too weighty for the relatively banal content.

Gradatio or Climax: The word "climax" has become fully naturalized in
English, but in the process its meaning has been altered. Although in
Greek—and in rhetoric—"climax" means simply "ladder," in English we
understand the climax to be the top step, the ultimate point of the climb.
For this reason it is probably best to use the Latin name for the figure, *gradatio*. The steps in gradatio are successive clauses with a specific kind of repetition: the ending of the first clause becomes the beginning of the second
clause; the ending of the second clause becomes the beginning of the third;
and so on in series. A famous example comes from Shakespeare:

For your brother and my sister no sooner met but they looked; no
sooner looked but they loved, no sooner loved but they sighed; no

sooner sighed but they asked one another the reason; no sooner they knew the reason than they sought the remedy; and in these degrees have they made a pair of stairs to marriage.

Shakespeare, *As You Like It*, V.ii.36-42

Here Shakespeare not only uses a gradatio but, with the phrase "they made a pair of stairs," names the figure by building a concrete image of ascent.

Gradatio is particularly effective in expressing a linked chain of events, as in a series of causes and effects:

Criticism based on verisimilitude is very fond of "evident truths." These evident truths are, however, essentially normative. By a habitual process of confused logic, the unbelievable proceeds from the forbidden, that is to say from the dangerous: disagreements become divergences, divergences become errors, errors become sins, sins become illnesses, illnesses become monstrosities.

Roland Barthes, *Criticism and Truth*, translated by Philip Thody, 35-6

The same figure can also be used in a different form:

In the histories of art and literature the eighteenth century is credited as the common sense age and the nineteenth as the time of romance, but this hardly holds for the folk traditions. The formalized, marine-pastoral air of the old sailor songs gave way to realism and irony in the later days of sail, when capitalist competition and the need to fulfill sailing schedules on time meant that the working of ships became more intense, with the mate driving the men, the skipper driving the mate, the company driving the skipper.

A.L. Lloyd, *Folk Song in England*, 263

The ending of the passage gives the sense of a chain, but the sequence is "mate . . . men," "skipper . . . mate," "company . . . skipper," as the beginning of one clause becomes the end of the next. This figure is more like playing leap-frog than climbing a ladder.

6

MORE FIGURES

Zeugma: When a single verb is used in more than one sense, particularly when it takes one object in the first sense and another object in the second, the figure is called *zeugma*. For example:

> Charles the Bold set out with a magnificent army of nobles to force the resisting confederates into submission to his empire. Near Murten he lost his cavalry, near Granson his artillery, and near Nancy his life.

> Otto Zierer, *A History of Germany*, translated by G. Irvins, 49

Here the verb "to lose" is taken in two different senses, with two different objects: to lose cavalry or artillery is to misplace them; to lose one's life is to die. Zeugma is clever; its effect is usually a sort of intellectual shock:

> Doña Ester had begun to suffer from arthritis at an early age, becoming stiffer and stiffer until she could only move with the greatest difficulty, like a living corpse; finally, no longer able to bend her knees, she had settled for good into her wheelchair, her widow-hood, and her despair.

> Isabel Allende, *The House of the Spirits*, 45

These two passages happen to come from German and Spanish, translated into English; I don't know whether these zeugmata are in the original versions or have been introduced by the translators. I suspect that different languages offer different opportunities for zeugma, as they do for puns. In any event, here is an example that was written in English:

> President Washington immediately summoned his Cabinet, together with high Pennsylvania authorities, to consider the critical situation

in the West. The President himself opened the meeting by declaring that the disorders in the West struck at the very roots of law and order and that "the most spirited & firm measures were necessary: if such proceedings were tolerated there was an end to our Constitution." But when he asked Governor Mifflin to aid in suppressing the uprising, the governor seemed far more eager to raise objections than to raise troops.

John C. Miller, *Alexander Hamilton and the Growth of the New Nation*, 406

In the first two examples, from Otto Zierer and Isabel Allende, the more literal sense of the verb comes first, followed by the more abstract meaning: Charles the Bold lost his cavalry and his artillery, then his life; Dona Ester settled into her wheelchair, then into her widowhood and her despair. Following that pattern would improve the third example: "But when he asked Governor Mifflin to aid in suppressing the uprising, the governor seemed far less eager to raise troops than to raise objections."

Tricolon: The human tendency to compose groups of three has often been noticed—in characters (three sons in folktales; three suitors in *The Portrait of a Lady*); in words ("her wheelchair, her widowhood, and her despair"); and in phrases ("near Murten he lost his cavalry, near Granson his artillery, and near Nancy his life"). A tripling of phrases, clauses, or sentences is called *tricolon*; if the phrases are arranged so that they progressively increase in length, the figure is called *tricolon crescendo*:

> The year 1880 . . . was to prove to be the most retentive and talented one in his long, too long, never too long life.

Vladimir Nabokov, *Ada*, 171

Of course pairs are also very common, but triples are more noticeable. Triple rhythm is pleasant for writers and readers alike, especially when the elements increase in length and weight. Hence the impulse to compose in tricolon crescendo is strong, and sometimes the result can seem a bit mechanical. In the next passage the word "mortal" adds little to the meaning, but it does lengthen the third colon:

Why and for how long? An innocent, childlike question that other Ephraims throughout the generations have never stopped asking. The Romans and the enemies of the Romans, the Christians and the enemies of the Christians, the Moslems and the mortal enemies of Islam: Ephraim was everyone's favorite target.

Elie Wiesel, *A Beggar in Jerusalem*, 112

The next passage concerns Maecenas, a friend and associate of the emperor Augustus. Maecenas was the most important literary patron of his time, but he was not successful in his own literary efforts:

It is probably impossible to overstate the debt of the Augustan régime to the literary taste and genius for friendship of the complicated Maecenas. When, after his breach with Maecenas, Augustus took literary patronage into his own hands, the immediate result was the pressuring of Horace and apparently of Propertius, the more distant the banishment of Ovid, and the ultimate outcome several generations' silence. If the Augustan régime cuts a good figure in great literature, one can hardly except as a reason the protection that Maecenas afforded his poets. He chose them with a taste that failed only, and failed signally, to correct his own writings, he gave them financial independence if they needed it, and he left them to follow their own bent.

Margaret Hubbard, *Propertius*, 99

The first tricolon is organized chronologically ("immediate," "more distant," and "ultimate"), and although the elements do not increase in length, the results become more serious ("pressuring," "banishment," "silence"). The second tricolon actually shows a steady decrease in length:

(1) He chose them with a taste that failed only, and failed signally, to correct his own writings,
(2) he gave them financial independence if they needed it,
(3) and he left them to follow their own bent.

I think this sequence could be improved. The comment about Maecenas' own writings is not really necessary here; and if the last element is the most

important, it should be marked in some way. A possible revision might run
as follows:

(1) He chose them with unerring taste,

(2) he gave them financial independence if they needed it,

(3) and what is most important, he left them alone to follow their
own bent.

The next passage shows the power of rhetoric in the hands of a great
rhetorician. The ending is a tricolon crescendo (with polysyndeton and also
a polyptoton in "glorious/glory"):

> I was always embarrassed by the words sacred, glorious, and sacrifice
> and the expression in vain. We had heard them sometimes standing
> in the rain almost out of earshot, so that only the shouted words
> came through, and had read them, on proclamations that were
> slapped up by billporters over other proclamations, now for a long
> time, and I had seen nothing sacred, and the things that were glori-
> ous had no glory and the sacrifices were like the stockyards at
> Chicago if nothing was done with the meat except to bury it.

> Ernest Hemingway, *A Farewell to Arms*, 184-5

The end of the passage picks up three terms from the beginning, "the words
sacred, glorious, and sacrifice":

> I had seen nothing sacred
> and the things that were glorious had no glory
> and the sacrifices were like the stockyards at Chicago if nothing was
> done with the meat except to bury it.

The tricolon at the end leaves out the fourth term, "the expression in vain,"
but it's hardly needed: the image that concludes the paragraph implicitly
makes the point.

Chiasmus: The name of this figure comes from the shape of the Greek letter *chi*, which is like our letter "x." Four terms are involved, in this order:

A1   B1
B2   A2

If one line connected the As and another line connected the Bs, the two lines would form an "x." Of course this vertical arrangement has to be imagined, since the words of the sentence will actually come in linear order:

Value-judgements are founded on the study of literature; the study of literature can never be founded on value-judgements.

Northrop Frye, *The Anatomy of Criticism*, 20

Here A1 and A2 are "value-judgements," while B1 and B2 are "the study of literature." The vertical arrangement would be:

value judgements / the study of literature
the study of literature / value judgements

Chiasmus, like zeugma, is clever. It is particularly appropriate to a certain style of intellectual disputation, and has been popular in recent academic writing. Frye uses chiasmus twice again within a few pages of the passage just quoted:

The axiom of criticism must be, not that the poet does not know what he is talking about, but that he cannot talk about what he knows.

Frye, *The Anatomy of Criticism*, 5

It is still possible for a critic to define as authentic art whatever he happens to like, and to go on to assert that what he happens not to like is, in terms of that definition, not authentic art.

Frye, *The Anatomy of Criticism*, 26

Examples of chiasmus are easy to find. Here are two more:

[Yeats] spent much of his life attempting to understand the deep contradictions within his mind, and was perhaps most alive to that which separated the man of action lost in reverie from the man of reverie who could not quite find himself in action.

Richard Ellman, *Yeats: The Man and the Masks*, 2

Great painters are often less skillful than mediocre painters; it is their concept of painting, not their skills, that defines their activities. Similarly, a foreigner may be less skillful than a native speaker at manipulating tenses or using subjunctives, but nonetheless be an incomparably better writer. Intellectual activities generate skills, but skills do not generate intellectual activities.

Francis-Noël Thomas and Mark Turner, *Clear and Simple as the Truth*, 4

The popularity of chiasmus in some academic circles derives from the title of a book by Karl Marx. The French anarchist Pierre-Joseph Proudhon wrote a book titled *System of Economic Contradictions, or the Philosophy of Poverty* (in French, *Système des contradictions économiques, ou la philosophie de la misère*). Marx wrote a critique, which he titled *The Poverty of Philosophy, a Response to the Philosophy of Poverty* by M. Proudhon (*Misère de la philosophie. Réponse à la "Philosophie de la misère" de M. Proudhon*). These models have inspired many similar titles: "Poetry of Grammar and Grammar of Poetry," "Fiction as Interpretation/Interpretation as Fiction," "Structure of Ideology and Ideology of Structure."[1]

In the examples quoted so far, the terms of the chiasmus have been identical (value-judgements / the study of literature // the study of literature / value-judgements, or philosophy / poverty // poverty / philosophy), but identity is not required. The terms can be varied so that A1 is not exactly the same as A2, nor B1 the same as B2. The following comes from a discussion of Melville's *Moby-Dick*:

For Ahab does not change; the action of the whole book, indeed, hardly moves for a while; there is only the long stretch of description, reverie, waiting, and then the fatal combat described in the last few chapters; a combat which we do not see approaching, which could only come suddenly, absent one moment, unconditionally present the next; neither to be courted in its absence, nor when it is there avoided.

Edwin Muir, *The Structure of the Novel*, 69

In the final chiasmus, A1 is "courted," A2 is "avoided"; B1 is "absence," B2 is "when it is there":

courted / absence
when it is there / avoided.

One term in each pair is positive, the other is negative, and the single word "absence" is matched by the phrase "when it is there." Muir's decision to vary the terms of this chiasmus was probably wise, given that the previous clause had used the words "absent" and "present": "absent one moment, unconditionally present the next." Without the variation we would read "absent one moment, unconditionally present the next; neither to be courted in its absence, nor in its presence avoided."

Marx used chiasmus to express bitter scorn, but its more usual functions are simply to avoid the boredom of an obvious parallelism, and especially to create effective emphasis at the end:

In a much larger sense, what Sterne parodied was rhetoric, not Fielding and Smollet, two thousand years of solemn theory, not twenty years of prose fiction.

Philip Stevick, *The Chapter in Fiction*, 170

The passage is not faulty as it stands, but chiasmus might improve it. A1 is "rhetoric," B1 is "Fielding and Smollett"; A2 is "two thousand years of solemn theory," B2 is "twenty years of prose fiction":

In a much larger sense, what Sterne parodied was rhetoric, not Fielding and Smollett: not twenty years of prose fiction, but two thousand years of solemn theory.

Or, in another variation:

In a much larger sense, what Sterne parodied was not Fielding and Smollet, but rhetoric: two thousand years of solemn theory, not twenty years of prose fiction.

The final sentence of the following passage has two clauses, which end almost identically:

> Habsburg creativeness was exhausted with the failure of Charles V. In 1556, when he abdicated and the Imperial title passed to Ferdinand, began the Habsburg struggle to survive in greatness; the Habsburg monarchy had acquired its lasting character. External enemies had been the danger of the first half of the sixteenth century; disintegration was the danger of the second half of the century.

> > A.J. Taylor, *The Habsburg Monarchy: 1809–1918*, 13-14

The point of the last sentence lacks force, but chiasmus could remedy the problem: "External enemies had been the danger of the first half of the sixteenth century; the danger of the second half was disintegration."

> This humanistic attack on the anthropomorphic ("man-locked") intelligence fosters techniques of perception which are dissociative rather than associative in nature. They do not make the strange familiar but rather estrange the familiar.

> > Geoffrey H. Hartman, *Beyond Formalism: Literary Essays 1958–1970*, 66

Chiasmus can prevent the jingle of "strange / familiar // estrange / familiar": "they do not make the strange familiar but rather make the familiar strange." Another possibility: "they do not familiarize the strange but rather estrange the familiar."

Of course chiasmus is not always the best choice. The following passage is intensely lyrical to begin with, and the final chiasmus tips the balance towards excess:

> Their bodies, corpse white or suffused with a pallid golden light or rawly tanned by the sun, gleamed with the wet of the sea. Their

diving stone, poised on its rude supports and rocking under their plunges, and the rough hewn stones of the sloping breakwater over which they scrambled in their horseplay, gleamed with cold wet lustre. The towels with which they smacked their bodies were heavy with seawater; and drenched with brine was their matted hair.

James Joyce, A Portrait of the Artist as a Young Man, 168

The natural order seems as good, or even better: "the towels with which they smacked their bodies were heavy with seawater; and their matted hair was drenched with brine."

Although chiasmus normally works with four items, more complex patterns can be created if there is more than one term:

The prescribers for the literature of the future usually cherish some great figure of the past whom they regard as having fulfilled their conditions and whom they are always bringing forward to demonstrate the inferiority of the literature of the present. As there has never existed a great writer who really had anything in common with these critics' conception of literature, they are obliged to provide imaginary versions of what their ideal great writers are like. The Humanists had Sophocles and Shakespeare; the socialist realists had Tolstoy. Yet it is certain that if Tolstoy had had to live up to the objectives and prohibitions which the socialist realists proposed he could never have written a chapter; and that if Babbitt and More had been able to enforce against Shakespeare their moral and esthetic injunctions he would never have written a line.

Edmund Wilson, "Marxism and Literature," in
The Triple Thinkers, 207–8

The ending of this passage deploys several elements in varying patterns. First there is a parallel construction:

The Humanists had Sophocles and Shakespeare;
the socialist realists had Tolstoy.

Then Wilson repeats these terms, but in a different order: Tolstoy, socialist realists, Babbitt and More (= the Humanists), Shakespeare. And he introduces new terms: "objectives and prohibitions," "moral and esthetic injunctions"; "written a chapter," "written a line." The elements are (A) critical school; (B) writer; (C) standard of evaluation; (D) literary product. From "the Humanists" to the end, the order is as follows:

> (A1) The Humanists had (B1) Sophocles and Shakespeare; (A2) the socialist realists had (B2) Tolstoy. Yet it is certain that if (B2) Tolstoy had had to live up to the (C1) objectives and prohibitions which (A2) the socialist realists proposed he could never have (D1) written a chapter; and that if (A1) Babbitt and More had been able to enforce against (B1) Shakespeare their (C2) moral and esthetic injunctions he would never have (D2) written a line.

Or, in graphic form:

> A1 / B1
> A2 / B2
> B2 / C1 / A2 / D1
> A1 / B1 / C2 / D2

A rearrangement could avoid the parallel position of D1 and D2; and perhaps the D elements are not the most emphatic endings. But I don't mean to be over-critical; I like the passage as it stands.

An Unnamed Figure: In this section I have collected a few examples of a distinctive and useful construction that has remained so far as I know unnamed. This structure is a comparison involving four terms—A is to B as C is to D—in which one of the terms of the second half is special in some way. Here is an example:

> The only way to forestall the work of criticism is through censorship, which has the same relationship to criticism that lynching has to justice.
>
> Northrop Frye, *The Anatomy of Criticism*, 4

Censorship is to criticism as lynching is to justice. The point here is to invest censorship with all the bad feelings we have about lynching, while investing criticism with all the good feelings we have about justice. But it's really the word "lynching" that does the job. Frye rather likes this figure; here is another example:

> The history of taste is no more a part of the structure of criticism than the Huxley-Wilberforce debate is part of the structure of biological science.
>
> Northrop Frye, *The Anatomy of Criticism*, 18

Again the point lies in the third item: in 1860, the biologist T.H. Huxley publicly debated the new theory of natural selection with Bishop Samuel Wilberforce. The debate had its importance in the public acceptance of Darwin's theory, but it wasn't science. The history of taste is equally peripheral. Frye, however, proposes a kind of criticism that would have the dignity of *On the Origin of Species*.

The next example varies the figure somewhat, so that it is the fourth term of the proportion which is emphatic:

> It is the nature of words to mean. To consider words only as sounds, like drum taps, or to consider written letters as patterned objects, as in alphabet soup, is the same as to consider a Stradivarius as material for kindling wood.
>
> William Wimsatt, *The Prose Style of Samuel Johnson*, 3–4

Again there are four terms, but the first two terms are doubled: (A) words (B) sounds, like drum taps; (A2) letters (B2) patterned objects, like the noodles in alphabet soup; (C) a Stradivarius violin, (D) kindling wood. The outrage of reducing a Strad to kindling reinforces Wimsatt's point.

The argument of the next passage requires some explanation. The followers of Freud and Jung have used the study of myth as a part of psychotherapy; in so doing they have tended to reduce myth to pathology. Joseph Campbell, by contrast, argues that myth is not regressive, a return to infantile impulses, but progressive as it releases psychic energies and directs them into the field of adult experience and performance. If this process does not work, if an individual has suffered a psychic trauma, then

> a regressive interpretation of his peculiar mode of experiencing the imagery of local myth may be in order. However, for the psychoan-

alyst then to make use of the fantasies of that regressive case as a key to the scientific understanding of the progressively functioning mythology and ceremonialism of the social group in question would be about as appropriate as to mistake a pancake for a soufflé.

Joseph Campbell, *The Masks of God*, vol. 1, *Primitive Mythology*, 92

This example is complicated, but again there are four terms in the comparison: (A) myth regarded as regressive; (B) myth understood as progressive; (C) a pancake; (D) a soufflé. No doubt the simplicity of the third and fourth terms is intended to resolve some of the complexity: a pancake is what you get when a soufflé, instead of rising, falls flat.

One frequent feature of this unnamed figure is the comparison of something complex or abstract to something shocking or concrete or banal: lynching; kindling wood; a pancake. The value judgement implied by this second term is then transferred to the more abstract part of the comparison. The use of a strongly valued term in a comparison can be seen in other passages where the figure is not quite so fully developed as in the examples above:

A reader who quarrels with postulates, who dislikes Hamlet because he does not believe that there are ghosts or that people speak in pentameters, clearly has no business in literature. He cannot distinguish fiction from fact, and belongs in the same category as the people who send cheques to radio stations for the relief of suffering heroines in soap operas.

Northrop Frye, *The Anatomy of Criticism*, 76

We can easily see the stupidity of people who send money to soap opera heroines; people who reject literary conventions are just as stupid.

So far as I know, there is no name in rhetoric for this sort of construction based on a strongly valued concrete term; nor is there a name for the sort of comparison that depends on such a term. No doubt there are enough rhetorical terms already, and I don't propose to add new ones. But these figures exist all the same, and other unnamed figures as well. Named or not, they are all resources for the writer.

7

PARALLELISM AND ANTITHESIS

Parallelism is more than a figure of speech, it is a principle of composition: that similar ideas should be expressed in similar form. Similarity of construction is a formal indication of similar ideas. The parallelism principle extends to antithesis, which is the parallel construction of contrasting ideas. The parallels can be as short as individual words or as long as chapters or even whole sections of a book. The plot of *Women in Love*, for example, can be considered a prolonged parallel of the romantic lives of the two sisters, Ursula and Gudrun.

Parallelism is frequent both in the curt and pointed Senecan style and in the more longwinded style derived from Cicero. But not every style aims for parallelism, and not every writer favors the principle. The Greek historian Thucydides often deliberately violated parallel structure; and later I will give some examples of nonparallel structure in modern writers. Some writers, without deliberately violating the principle of parallelism, appear to have no particular use for it. In fact, there is relatively little parallelism in most modern narratives, perhaps because the structure of ideas is not the point of the fiction. On the other hand, some writers seem to create verbal parallels and antitheses even when the subject they are writing about does not appear to demand such treatment. Parallelism occurs in every age, but it is perhaps most characteristic of eighteenth-century writers such as Henry Fielding, Samuel Johnson, David Hume, and Edward Gibbon.[1]

In a sense, any linking of words in corresponding syntax forms a parallel. In the sentence "He bought butter and eggs," the words "butter" and "eggs" are both direct objects of the verb and to that extent they are parallel; but the parallel is weak, and this would hardly be a useful example. Very little is needed, however, to create a noticeable instance of parallelism. In *A Journey From This World to the Next*, Fielding presents a conversation among the souls of some people recently dead, one of whom was killed in a duel:

The gentleman who died of honour very liberally cursed both his folly and his fencing.

Henry Fielding, *A Journey from this World to the Next*, 11

The grammar here is the same as in the butter-and-eggs example: "folly" and "fencing" are both direct objects of the verb; but the parallel is brought out by the word "both" and perhaps even more by the alliteration. The parallel is not exact: the gentleman no doubt cursed his folly in agreeing to the duel and also cursed the poor quality of his fencing. But this inexact parallel is a better example of the construction than the exact but weak parallel of "butter and eggs."

Parallels between single words may be emphasized by accumulation. The next passage has two antithetical pairs:

I now fell into the hands of one of a very different disposition, and this was no other than the celebrated St. Chrysostom, who dieted me with sermons instead of sacrifices, and filled my ears with good things, but not my belly.

Henry Fielding, *A Journey from this World to the Next*, 48

The two antitheses here make the same point, but accumulation (in this case, doubling) gives emphasis to both the idea and the construction. The first antithesis—marked by alliteration—consists in one direct object ("me") and two antithetical prepositional phrases ("with sermons" and "instead of sacrifices"). The second antithesis varies the grammar: here we have one prepositional phrase ("with good things") and two antithetical direct objects ("my ears" and "not my belly"); and the strongest element is kept for the end.

Parallels become more noticeable when they become more complex. Even single words, to be sure, have some features that can be used to emphasize the construction (such as the alliteration in "folly" and "fencing," or "sermons" and "sacrifice"); phrases, however, offer more elements to play with:

We found his lordship sitting at the upper end of a table, on which was an immense sum of money, disposed in several heaps, every one of which would have purchased the honour of some patriots and the chastity of some prudes.

Henry Fielding, *A Journey from this World to the Next*, 14

In the earlier examples "folly" was parallel to "fencing" and "sermons" was parallel to "sacrifices"; here "honour of some patriots" is parallel to "chastity of some prudes." The phrases are parallel not only because they are both objects of the verb, but also because they have the same internal structure. The more elements in a construction, the more noticeable the parallel.

Both accumulation and complication can be used in a single passage:

To say the truth, between my solicitude in contriving schemes to procure money and my extreme anxiety in preserving it, I never had one moment of ease while awake nor of quiet when in my sleep.

Henry Fielding, *A Journey from this World to the Next*, 56

These parallels show some variation: the single word "solicitude" is matched by the two-word phrase "extreme anxiety"; "in contriving schemes to procure money" is longer than "in preserving it." Making the parallels more exact ("between my solicitude in procuring money and my anxiety in preserving it") would not make them any better. The second parallel—"ease while awake" / "quiet when in my sleep"—is more nearly exact, but here too Fielding has allowed himself some variation. There is no rule; the writer must decide (and the reader may judge) whether the parallel should be exact or varied.

Parallelism tends to be analytical and intellectual rather than emotional. It is the result of the examination and comparison of two or more different things—objects, events, people, ideas—and then the recognition that they have the same structure. In scientific writing, the accumulation of evidence to prove a point often lends itself to parallelism:

Although I do not doubt that some domestic animals vary less than others, yet the rarity or absence of distinct breeds of the cat, the donkey, peacock, goose, &c., may be attributed in main part to selection not having been brought into play: in cats, from the difficulty in pairing them; in donkeys, from only a few being kept by poor people, and little attention being paid to their breeding; for recently in certain parts of Spain and of the United States this animal has been surprisingly modified and improved by careful selection; in peacocks, from not being very easily reared and a large stock not kept; in geese, from being valuable only for two purposes, food and feathers, and more especially from no pleasure having been felt in the display of distinct breeds; but the goose, under the conditions to which it is exposed when domesticated, seems to have a singularly inflexible organization, though it has varied to a slight extent, as I have elsewhere described.

Charles Darwin, *On the Origin of Species*, 62

This long sentence is part of Darwin's discussion of artificial selection (the selection, by breeders, of favoured individual domestic animals). In the first part he names four species—cat, donkey, peacock, and goose—to be discussed in successive sections of the sentence. Each of these sections begins in the same way, but they continue quite variously: in cats, from (A); in donkeys, from (B); in peacocks, from (C); in geese, from (D). "A" is a phrase 5 words long; "B" has three parts, of 8, 8, and 23 words; "C" is a co-ordinated phrase 11 words long; and "D" divides into two major parts, of 23 and 33 words, each of which could be further subdivided. A careful balance of parallelism and variation shows the reader just what is similar and what is different in these four cases. Darwin frequently used parallel constructions, some longer and more complex than the passage quoted here. Indeed, his intellect was essentially comparative; he saw the world as a vast set of parallels, and he had at hand grammatical structures well suited to his ideas.

Historians as well as scientists often frame their thoughts in parallel constructions:

In the ancient world everyone knew at least three things about the Jews: they would not be associated either directly or indirectly with any pagan cult (which seemed antisocial), they refused to eat not only meat that had been offered in sacrifice to the gods but also all pork (which seemed ridiculous), and they circumcised their male infants (which seemed repulsive).

Henry Chadwick, *The Early Church*, 18–19

What "everyone" knew about the Jews and what "everyone" felt—these are matters of historical fact or judgment. But the organization of such facts and judgments into two series of three parallels, this is the product of the writer's mental action.

Parallels may also be found in the world of the mind or the emotions. Here David Hume considers whether moral judgments are founded on reason or on sentiment:

> Truth is disputable, not taste: what exists in the nature of things is the standard of our judgement; what each man feels within himself is the standard of sentiment. Propositions in geometry may be proved, systems in physics may be controverted; but the harmony of verse, the tenderness of passion, the brilliancy of wit, must give immediate pleasure.

> David Hume, *An Enquiry Concerning the Principles of Morals*, 3

Hume is not satisfied with this argument, which he states only so that he can refute it. The point is that the parallels in the passage are parallels Hume has discovered through thought. After all, much of what is interesting about the world is interpretation rather than fact. A similarity of structure may be inherent in whatever the writer has observed, but it may also be created, at least in part, by the way the writer sees. It may even be an act of will, an imposition on the world of an idea already established in the mind of the writer:

> It is reasonable to suppose that it is just as hard for rich people grown poor to believe in their poverty as it is for poor people turned rich to believe in their wealth; the former seem carried away by a recklessness of which they are totally unaware, the latter seem possessed by a stinginess which actually is nothing but the old ingrained fear of what the next day may bring.

> Hannah Arendt, "Introduction" to *Illuminations*, by Walter Benjamin

Arendt begins with a complex parallel construction of antitheses:

> rich people / grown poor / believe / in their poverty
> poor people / turned rich / believe / in their wealth

Next comes a parallel of four terms, with a longer colon at the end to provide the climax:

former / carried away by / recklessness / of which they are totally unaware
latter / possessed by / stinginess / which actually is nothing but the old ingrained fear of what the next day may bring.

The basis of the proposition is the division of the world into the rich and the poor. This division is commonplace, but of course it is a simplification. Arendt adopts it not so much because it is true as because it allows her to construct the parallel. Nor does the value of the parallel itself lie in its truth: it is too general to be either true or false. What Arendt proposes here is not really an argument, but a way of looking at the world.

In ancient Rome, powerful men gathered around themselves subordinates who were called clients; the more clients a patron had, the more power he could demonstrate to society:

The life of a "client" was horrible: without self-respect, without hope of independence unless after long servitude, without any real leisure, and without any real work—a lifetime of standing in waiting-rooms and loitering in corridors and bowing to blind eyes and begging for petty favors, the friend of a man who was neither your equal nor your companion, the dependent of a man who treated you as a useless ornament, the flatterer of a man whom you hated and who usually knew it.

Gilbert Highet, *Juvenal the Satirist*, 7

Highet's description is based on fact, but it is also a selection, an interpretation, an ordering: in short, a work of art. After an introductory clause—"The life of a 'client' was horrible"—the rest of the passage is organized in three sets of parallels. The first four items all begin with the same preposition:

without self-respect
without hope of independence unless after long servitude
without any real leisure
without any real work

The second four all begin with a gerund followed by a prepositional phrase:

> standing in waiting-rooms
> loitering in corridors
> bowing to blind eyes
> begging for petty favors

And the last three all begin with a noun followed by a prepositional phrase and a relative clause:

> the friend of a man who was neither your equal nor your companion,
> the dependent of a man who treated you as a useless ornament,
> the flatterer of a man whom you hated and who usually knew it.

Parallels are constructed not only by scientists, philosophers, and historians, but also by novelists, at least those of an analytical frame of mind:

> Elizabeth, on her side, had much to do. She wanted to ascertain the feelings of each of her visitors; she wanted to compose her own, and to make herself agreeable to all; and in the latter object, where she feared most to fail, she was most sure of success, for those to whom she endeavoured to give pleasure were prepossessed in her favour. Bingley was ready, Georgiana was eager, and Darcy was determined to be pleased.

Jane Austen, Pride and Prejudice, Chapter 44

Most of this passage consists of parallels: Elizabeth

> wanted to ascertain the feelings of each of her visitors; she
> wanted to compose her own, and
>   to make herself agreeable to all; where
> she feared most to fail,
> she was most sure of success
> Bingley was ready,
> Georgiana was eager, and
> Darcy was determined to be pleased.

Even more extensive parallelism can be found in the passage from Lyly's *Euphues* that we have already looked at:

> There dwelt in Athens a young gentleman of great patrimony, & of so comely a personage, that it was doubted whether he were more bound to Nature for the lineaments of his person, or to Fortune for the increase of his possessions. But Nature impatient of comparisons, and as it were disdaining a companion, or copartner in her working, added to this comeliness of his body such a sharp capacity of mind, that not only she proved Fortune counterfeit, but was half of that opinion that she herself was only current. This young gallant, of more wit than wealth, and yet of more wealth than wisdom, seeing himself inferior to none in pleasant conceits, thought himself superior to all in honest conditions, insomuch that he deemed himself so apt to all things, that he gave himself almost to nothing, but practicing of those things commonly which are incident to these sharp wits, fine phrases, smooth quipping, merry taunting, using jesting without mean, & abusing mirth without measure.

> John Lyly, *Euphues: The Anatomy of Wit*, 91

Many of the parallels here are complex. By itself the phrase "more wit than wealth" is a parallel antithesis of the two nouns, marked by alliteration, but this parallelism is then extended by the phrase "more wealth than wisdom," a parallel antithesis that is antithetically parallel to the first antithesis, marked by the same alliteration, and embellished with a small gradatio, as the last term of the first colon becomes the first term of the second colon. Euphues is indebted to "Nature for the lineaments of his person" and to "Fortune for the increase of his possessions"; here three terms in the first colon are parallel to three terms in the second: Nature / Fortune; lineaments / increase; person / possessions.

Extended exercises in parallelism can be found in writers from the classical period to our own time. In the following excerpt from the ancient Greek romance *Leucippe and Clitophon*, the hero describes his first entry into the great city of Alexandria:

I tried to cast my eyes down every street, but my gaze was still unsatisfied, and I could not grasp all the beauty of the spot at once; some parts I saw, some I was on the point of seeing, some I could not pass by; that which I actually saw kept my gaze fixed, while that which I expected to see would drag it on to the next. I explored therefore every street, and at last, my vision unsatisfied, exclaimed in weariness, "Ah, my eyes, we are beaten." Two things struck me as especially strange and extraordinary—it was impossible to decide which was the greatest, the size of the place or its beauty, the city itself or its inhabitants; for the former was larger than a continent, the latter outnumbered a whole nation. Looking at the city, I doubted whether any race of men could ever fill it; looking at the inhabitants, I wondered whether any city could ever be found large enough to hold them all. The balance seemed exactly even.

> Achilles Tatius, *Leucippe and Clitophon*, Book V, Chapter 1;
> translated by S. Gaselee

For modern tastes the parallelism here may be excessive, but there is a great vigor and pleasure in the writing. This passage must have been fun to compose, and for the reader in the right frame of mind, it's still a lot of fun to read. In this sort of style, the figure doesn't merely serve the ideas; it becomes an end in itself, and ideas are sought to provide an occasion for the figure.

Extremes of parallelism are not confined to ancient or Renaissance literature; the following remarkable passage comes from Shaw's *Man and Superman*:

THE DEVIL [*mortified*]: Señor Don Juan: you are uncivil to my friends.

DON JUAN: Pooh! why should I be civil to them or to you? In this Palace of Lies a truth or two will not hurt you. Your friends are all the dullest dogs I know. They are not beautiful: they are only decorated. They are not clean: they are only shaved and starched. They are not dignified: they are only fashionably dressed. They are not educated: they are only college passmen. They are not religious: they are only pewrenters. They are not moral: they are only conventional. They are not virtuous: they are only cowardly. They are not even vicious: they are only "frail." They are not artists: they are only lascivious. They are not prosperous: they are only rich. They are not loyal, they are only servile; not dutiful, only sheepish; not public spirited, only patriotic; not courageous, only quarrelsome; not determined, only obstinate; not masterful, only domineering; not self-controlled, only obtuse; not self-respecting, only vain; not kind, only sentimental; not social, only gregarious; not considerate, only polite; not intelligent, only opinionated; not progressive, only factious; not imaginative, only superstitious; not just, only vindictive; not generous, only propitiatory; not disciplined, only cowed; and not truthful at all: liars every one of them, to the very backbone of their souls.

George Bernard Shaw, *Man and Superman*, Act III

This speech has a certain impressiveness, but it just goes on too long. Shaw varies the rhythm—first by dropping the subject pronoun, and then by expanding the structure at the end—but more help is needed to defeat the monotony. The dramatic effect of the passage might be improved if it were divided between two people, as follows:

DON JUAN: Your friends are the dullest dogs I know.
THE DEVIL: But they are beautiful.
DON JUAN: No, they are only decorated.
THE DEVIL: But they are dignified.
DON JUAN: No, they are only fashionably dressed.
THE DEVIL: They are educated.
DON JUAN: They are only college passmen.
THE DEVIL: They are artistic.
DON JUAN: They are only lascivious.
THE DEVIL: They are prosperous.
DON JUAN: They are only rich.
THE DEVIL: They are loyal.
DON JUAN: They are only servile.
THE DEVIL: They are clean.
DON JUAN: Only shaved and starched.

THE DEVIL: They are moral.
DON JUAN: Conventional.
THE DEVIL: Religious.

And so on. In this form, the monologue becomes a battle that might help the audience stay awake—though the ping-pong effect could itself become tedious.

The latter examples are extremes; the following passage is more modest, but still it gains some of its effect from its length:

Resuming his self-examination, he admitted that he had been a bad husband—twice. Daisy, his first wife, he had treated miserably. Madeleine, his second, had tried to do *him* in. To his son and his daughter he was a loving but bad father. To his own parents he had been an ungrateful child. To his country, an indifferent citizen. To his brothers and sisters, affectionate but remote. With his friends, an egoist. With love, lazy. With brightness, dull. With power, passive. With his own soul, evasive.

Saul Bellow, *Herzog*, 11–12

As in the Shaw monologue, the parallels here are short. The effect is a great heap of figures, piled up like grains of sand. There is no organization within the heap, and one parallel more or less would hardly be noticed. But parallel structure can also be used to organize larger structures of ideas. In the following passage, contrasting the achievements of Greek culture in the early eighth and the early seventh centuries BCE, the parallels are not simply decorative: they are the analytical framework that structures the entire paragraph:

Before this episode, the Greek world was an enclave whose boundaries hardly extended beyond Rhodes or Ithaka to the east and west, Macedonia and Crete to the north and south; the tentative contacts with southern Italy and the Levant had, as yet, no significant effect for anyone. After it, colonization and commerce had between them taken Greeks, repeatedly or even permanently, to the south of Spain, to Italy and Sicily, to North Africa, to the coast and even the hinterland of the Levant; the Greeks of Cyprus, isolated for so long, had been brought back into the cultural commonwealth. Before it, the low population and cultural level of the Greeks had made them certainly an obscure and perhaps even a backward people by the standards of the Mediterranean world; by its end, they were conspicuous everywhere as leaders and innovators. Before, they had been just another tribal society with fond memories of a better past; after, they were the expansive prophets of a new political system whose future must have seemed very bright. Before, they had orally-transmitted poetry of uncertain content and variable antiquity, which they were unable to record permanently; after, they had the songs of Homer and the means to write them down.

Anthony Snodgrass, *Archaic Greece*, 47–8

Snodgrass has constructed four antitheses, all proving a single point: the advance in Greek culture in the archaic period. Each antithesis is structured around the words "before" and "after" (or, in one case, "by its end"):

(A1) Before, the Greek world was a small enclave
(B1) After, the Greek world extended to the south of Spain, Italy, Sicily, North Africa, and the Levant

(A2) Before, the Greeks were an obscure and backward people
(B2) by its end, they were leaders and innovators

(A3) Before, they were a tribal society with fond memories of a better past
(B3) after, they were the expansive prophets of a new political system

(A4) Before, they had orally-transmitted poetry which they were unable to record permanently
(B4) after, they had the songs of Homer and the means to write them down.

Constructions that could be parallel but are not fall into three categories. Sometimes a writer will simply miss a good opportunity to mark parallel ideas with parallel grammar. Sometimes a writer will try for a parallel that doesn't quite work. And sometimes a writer will decide that a possible parallel construction would be awkward.

In cases of the first type the missing parallel is often easy to supply:

> The changes brought about by the opening of the country to foreign trade resulted in the edicts on clothing being abolished and in the availability of cheap cotton goods.
>
> Louis Allen, *Japan: The Years of Triumph*, 36

There are two possibilities here: either "the edicts on clothing being abolished and cheap cotton goods becoming available" or, better, "the abolition of the edicts on clothing and the availability of cheap cotton goods."

Far more interesting are non-parallels of second type, the noble failures. The following passage ends with a complex parallel that might be better if it were simplified:

> From 1378 to 1381, the story of the French war is a dreary catalogue of ineptitudes, only relieved here and there by the unco-ordinated exploits of a few individuals. And the ineptitude was not one-sided —the French were unable to profit from English inefficiency. Of creditable individual exploits, the story of Sir Hugh Calverley is notable. Of disgraceful incidents, the expedition of Sir John Arundel is typical. As an example of unprofitable campaigning, the military career of the luckless John of Gaunt is outstanding.
>
> Harold F. Hutchinson, *The Hollow Crown*, 40

The third and fourth sentences both begin with an anaphoric preposition, but in the final sentence the prepositional phrase is delayed. These three sentences are built around three sets of parallels:

(A1) creditable individual exploits
(A2) disgraceful incidents
(A3) unprofitable campaigning

(B1) Sir Hugh Calverley
(B2) Sir John Arundel
(B3) John of Gaunt

(C1) notable
(C2) typical
(C3) outstanding

Sentence endings are usually emphatic, but the words in the C series aren't very important; it's the A series that matters. The inversion of the grammar is probably intended to emphasize the A series by bringing those words to the front; for my ear, however, the initial prepositional phrases are awkward. In normal form, the sentences would run as follows: "The story of Sir Hugh Calverley is a notable example of creditable individual exploits; the expedition of Sir John Arundel is typical of disgraceful incidents; the military career of the luckless John of Gaunt is an outstanding example of unprofitable campaigning." These statements could be streamlined, with variation of the last element to provide weight at the end: "Sir Hugh Calverley's individual exploits were creditable; Sir John Arundel's expedition was disgraceful; John of Gaunt's military career was an outstanding example of unprofitable campaigning." If the adjective describing John of Gaunt is to be retained, the word order of the last clause would have to be changed: "the military career of the luckless John of Gaunt was an outstanding example of unprofitable campaigning."

On other occasions, however, Hutchinson does write effective parallels:

> If villeins in the country and free labourers in the towns were to improve their respective lots, their only means of expression was that assembly which their masters would call a mob, that demonstration which the authorities would try to suppress as a riot, and that combination which the King's Council would try to crush as treason.
>
> Harold F. Hutchinson, *The Hollow Crown*, 50

The possibility of a good parallel can be seductive. At the beginning everything works well, all the ideas and terms fall into place; yet at the end the structure falls apart:

> Why has the discipline of classical studies, with what looks like reverse alchemy, seeking lead for gold, consistently favored the conversion of philosophy into the *history* of philosophy, rhetoric into the

history of rhetoric, texts into the *history* of texts, mythic narratives into *historical* "evidence"?

> John Peradotto, *Man in the Middle Voice: Name and Narration in the
> Odyssey*, 7 (Peradotto's italics)

The emphatic word is "history"; the repetition marks it sufficiently, and the italics are not necessary. The greater problem, however, is the failure of the parallel in the fourth phrase. The first three work well; it is plausible that the history of philosophy is inferior to philosophy itself, that the history of rhetoric is inferior to rhetoric, and that the history of texts is inferior to the texts themselves. But the relationship between mythic narrative and historical evidence is not clearly the same as the relationship between philosophy and the history of philosophy (and so on). It may well be a mistake to use myth as historical evidence, but not because the one is primary and the other secondary. The rhetorical parallel fails because the ideas are not parallel.

Similarly, the author of the next passage tries for parallel construction but can't quite make it work:

> . . . tempting as it may seem, narratology cannot be limited to narrative, just as poetics does not study just poetry, metrics meter, and logic language. In fact, metrics makes sense only when meter is contrasted to rhythm, and of course poetics handles much more than poetry, logic is not limited to the study of language, nor is philosophy merely the love of wisdom.

> Thomas Pavel, *The Poetics of Plot*, 15

The passage begins well, with the parallels narratology / narrative, poetics / poetry, and metrics / meter; logic and language are not etymologically parallel, and in fact the relation between the two is not simple, but the alliteration almost persuades the reader not to care. The second sentence then complicates one of these pairs by adding a contrasting term: metrics / meter / rhythm. One may wonder why the first pair, narratology / narrative, has been omitted. The variation in the next two clauses is probably wise, as a way of avoiding an excessive parallel; then a new pair, philosophy / love of wisdom, is introduced out of nowhere. The reader may feel cheated of a parallel in thought that the initially parallel grammar seemed to promise.

In the early twentieth century the politics of England changed dramatically. A part of the change was a Conservative rebellion against the Liberal policy of Irish Home Rule.

> [T]he Tory Rebellion was not merely a brutal attack upon an enfeebled opponent—that is to say, political; it was not merely the impassioned defense of impossible privileges—that is to say, economic; it was also, and more profoundly, the unconscious rejection of an established security.
>
> George Dangerfield, *The Strange Death of Liberal England*, 141

Twice Dangerfield sums up his descriptions in a single word—"political" and "economic." It is clever (and cynical) to say in a word that a brutal attack on an enfeebled opponent is politics, and that the impassioned defense of impossible privileges is economics. But the sentence falls a little flat all the same, because he has missed the opportunity to show his cleverness a third time. He needs a single word to categorize "the unconscious rejection of an established security"; perhaps "psychological" or "pathological" would do— or "neurotic" (which he has already used on the previous page): "it was also, and more profoundly, the unconscious rejection of an established security— that is to say, pathological." Varying the order in the final clause might add more point to the construction: "it was also, and more profoundly, pathological—the unconscious rejection of an established security."

Parallelism, like any figure, can cloy. The principle laid down at the beginning of this chapter—that similar ideas should be stated in similar form—may not be the highest wisdom, if the result would sounds obvious, trite, or contrived:

> In Mr. Dombey's thoughts, the whole of the original design of the novel is retraced. It is not a static view; the contest still continues. He has passed beyond Paul's death, the wreck of his marriage, his fallen fortunes.
>
> Kathleen Tillotson, "Dombey and Son," in A.E. Dyson, ed.,
> *Dickens*, 165

The parallel would be "He has passed beyond the death of his son, the wreck of his marriage, the fall of his fortunes." But this version sounds overly rhetorical for the context, so I would not revise. Nor would I change the next passage:

> There is little doubt that the ancient inhabitants of Western Europe as a whole differed from the Aryan successors in two important customs. They buried their dead, whereas the Aryans invariably used cremation; and they were organized in systems of matriarchies. Aryan culture is patriarchal to its foundations.
>
> Owen Barfield, *History in English Words*, 23

The obvious parallel would be "They buried their dead, whereas the Aryans invariably used cremation; and they were organized in systems of matriarchies, whereas Aryan culture is patriarchal to its foundations." There is no failure here; Barfield must simply have felt that variation was more effective than exact parallelism.

The following passage discusses four examples of a phenomenon, but the writer has quite deliberately varied the presentation:

> Now we may understand the popularity throughout this period of the pseudonym, for the pseudonym symbolized the duality which resulted from the dissociation of the personality. Consider the examples of Yeats's friends: W.K. Magee, George Russell, Oscar Wilde, and William Sharp. Magee's pseudonym, "John Eglinton," is explicable in terms of increased euphony or of a necessary reaction by a man of wide culture against the provincialism implied in the Irish name. With George Russell the pseudonym is carried a step further: "A. E." is derived from Aeon, a word which came to him in a vision as the name of the heavenly man, to whose state he aspired. Wilde, on leaving England, adopted the name of "Sebastian Melmoth," combining his sense of martyrdom and expiation, and eliminating "amiable, irrepressible Oscar," as he hoped, completely. In William Sharp, one of the most typical writers of the 'nineties, the pseudonym reached its furthest development. So seriously did Sharp take the pseudonym, so fully did he assume in 1894 the per-

sonality of "Fiona Macleod," that he wrote under her name books in a style different from his own, sent letters for her to friends in a feminine handwriting, complained to friends who wrote to her that they never wrote to him, and eventually almost collapsed under the strain of double life.

Richard Ellmann, *Yeats: The Man and the Masks*, 76–7

In each case Ellmann uses a different grammatical structure to introduce the writer's real name. In the first, the name is the possessive genitive modifying the subject of the sentence: "Magee's pseudonym. . . ." In the second, the name is the object of a loosely attached prepositional phrase: "With George Russell. . . ." In the third, the name is the subject of the sentence: "Wilde. . . ." In the fourth, the name is once again part of a prepositional phrase, but with a different preposition: "In William Sharp . . ." There are other differences as well; in the case of Sharp, for example, more information is provided, in two additional sentences. Ellmann must have felt that a parallel construction extended over four examples would have sounded stiff and awkward, and I think he was right.

8

PERIODIC SENTENCES

Our word *comma* is derived from the Greek verb "kopto" (κόπτω), "to cut off." A comma was a group of words—a verbal slice, as it were; then by extension the term came to designate the mark setting off a group of words. Originally, then, a comma was not a punctuation mark but (more or less) what we would call a phrase.[1] What we call a comma was the mark of a comma.

Likewise, our word *colon* is derived from the Greek "kolon" (κῶλον), which originally meant a limb, such as an arm or a leg, and then by extension the limb of a sentence, or something like what we might call a clause.[2] Again, the word we use to refer to a mark of punctuation originally referred to a group of words; what we call a colon was the mark of a colon.

And likewise, our word *period* is derived from the Greek "periodos" (περίοδος), which meant something that goes around in a circle, that rotates or recurs, such as a cycle or period of time. Aristotle used the word to refer to a sentence that in some way turns back on itself, for example in an antithesis.[3] But this use of the term seems peculiar to Aristotle; in later rhetorical theory, a period is a long sentence that uses grammatical subordination, especially to create some sort of suspense of meaning (we will look at some examples in a moment). So again, what we call a period (or what the English call a "full stop") was the mark of a period. Today we use a period to end a sentence.

Our word *sentence* comes from the Latin "sententia," meaning an opinion, a judgement, or a decision. We still use the word this way when we talk about the sentence imposed by a judge in court. Some writers have a habit of including short maxims, often at the end of a section: in the past, these maxims were called sentences. Shakespeare often ended a scene with some kind of general statement summing up the situation—in *Hamlet*, for example, the end of act 1, scene 2: "Foul deeds will rise, / Though all the world o'erwhelm them, to men's eyes"; or the end of act 3, scene 1: "Madness in great ones must not unwatched go"; or the end of act 3, scene 3: "My words fly up, my thoughts remain below. / Words without thoughts never to heaven go."[4]

As a mark of punctuation the period is used to end any kind of sentence—simple, compound, complex, even sentence fragments. As a term in rhetoric, however, a period is a particular kind of sentence: a long one, typically including grammatical subordination and intended to suspend meaning as long as possible. The periodic style was perfected by Greek and Latin writers; Cicero is famous for his periods, though he used other kinds of sentences equally well. But suspended grammar is easier in Latin and Greek than in English: in those inflected languages the verb, which usually completes the meaning of the sentence, may come at the end. A good Ciceronian period does not translate easily into English, as we can see from the following passage, the beginning of Cicero's defense of the poet Archias:

> Si quid est in me ingeni, quod sentio quam sit exiguum, aut si qua exercitatio dicendi, in qua me non infitior mediocriter esse versatum, aut si huiusce rei ratio aliqua ab optimarmum artium studiis ac disciplina profecta, a qua ego nullum confiteor aetatis meae tempus abhoruisse, earum rerum omnium vel in primis hic A. Licinius fructum a me repetere prope suo iure debet.

> Cicero, *Pro Archia Poeta Oratio*, 1

The following version attempts to retain something of the Latin word order:

> If there is in me any talent, which I realize how slight it is, or if any experience of speaking, in which I do not deny myself moderately engaged, or if any system of this matter derived from study and training of the best education, to which I admit no time of my life to have been averse, the fruit of all these first and foremost Aulus Licinius [Archias] in return from me nearly by his own right ought to seek.

This awkward rendering is translationese rather than English. In the Latin, the last word of the period is the main verb *debet*, "he ought." Everything before this verb is suspended, both the meaning and the grammar, and the sense of the period becomes clear only at the very end. There are many ways to suspend the meaning and grammar of a period. Here Cicero begins with a series of conditions; we will see examples of this technique in English. Another method is to elaborate the subject, especially through a series of adjectival subordinate clauses. Fundamental to the true Ciceronian period, however, is the postponement of some crucial word—usually the main verb or the subject—until the very end. Such postponement is not usually possible in English; consequently periodic elaboration to the right of the main verb is more common:

> She asked me why I would venture on such a step, without con-
> sulting her; she said her advice might have been civilly asked, if I was
> resolved not to have been guided by it. That, whatever opinion I
> might have conceived of her understanding, the rest of the world
> thought better of it. That I had never failed when I asked her coun-
> sel, nor ever succeeded without it;—with much more of the same
> kind, too tedious to mention; concluding that it was a monstrous
> behavior to desert my party and come over to the court.
>
> Henry Fielding, *A Journey from This World to the Next*, 118

Here the subject and verb "she said" are followed by three object clauses:[5]

> she said
> (1) her advice might have been civilly asked ...
> (2) That, whatever opinion I might have conceived of her under-
> standing, the rest of the world thought better of it.
> (3) That I had never failed when I asked her counsel, nor ever suc-
> ceeded without it ...

In Latin it would have been possible to begin the period with these object clauses and to end with the subject and main verb.

The following passage from *Mansfield Park* is another example of multiple object clauses following a verb:

> Scarcely had [Edmund Bertram] done regretting Mary Crawford,
> and observing to Fanny how impossible it was that he should ever
> meet with such another woman, before it began to strike him
> whether a very different kind of woman might not do just as well—
> or a great deal better; whether Fanny herself were not growing as

dear, as important to him in all her smiles, and all her ways, as Mary Crawford had ever been; and whether it might not be a possible, a hopeful undertaking to persuade her that her warm and sisterly regard for him would be foundation enough for wedded love.

Jane Austen, *Mansfield Park*, Chapter 48

In these passages from Fielding and Austen, the verb has three object clauses, but there is no theoretical limit to the elaboration:

He bid me observe it, and I should always find, that the calamities of life were shared among the upper and the lower part of mankind, but that the middle station had the fewest disasters, and was not exposed to so many vicissitudes as the higher or lower part of mankind. Nay, they were not subjected to so many distempers and uneasinesses either of body or mind as those were who, by vicious living, luxury, and extravagances on one hand, or by hard labour, want of necessaries, and mean or insufficient diet on the other hand, bring distempers on themselves by the natural consequences of their way of living; that the middle station of life was calculated for all kinds of virtues and all kinds of enjoyments; that peace and plenty were the handmaids of a middle fortune; that temperance, moderation, quietness, health, society, all agreeable diversions, and all desirable pleasures were the blessings attending the middle station of life; that this way men went silently and smoothly through the world, and comfortably out of it, not embarrassed with the labours of the hands or of the head, not sold to the life of slavery for daily bread, or harassed with perplexed circumstances, which rob the soul of peace, and the body of rest; not enraged with the passion of envy, or secret burning lust of ambition for great things; but in easy circumstances sliding gently through the world, and sensibly tasting the sweets of living, without the bitter, feeling that they are happy, and learning by every day's experience to know it more sensibly.

Daniel Defoe, *Robinson Crusoe*, 28–9

The verb "find" has six object clauses introduced by the subordinating conjunction "that," and several of these object clauses are further elaborated.

The following analysis shows only the major divisions:

He bid me observe it, and I should always find,
(1) that the calamities of life were shared among the upper and the lower part of mankind, but
(2) that the middle station had the fewest disasters ...
(3) that the middle station of life was calculated for all kinds of virtues and all kinds of enjoyments;
(4) that peace and plenty were the handmaids of a middle fortune;
(5) that temperance, moderation, quietness, health, society, all agreeable diversions, and all desirable pleasures were the blessings attending the middle station of life;
(6) that this way men went silently and smoothly through the world, and comfortably out of it. ...

Sentences elaborated to the right of the verb are not really Ciceronian periods because the meaning is multiplied rather than suspended—that is, the sentence would still have made sense if it had ended after the first object clause, but more objects have been added. The elaboration adds to the meaning, but it is not necessary to either the meaning or the grammar of the sentence. A true Ciceronian period is suspended because a crucial element of the sentence—usually either the subject or the main verb—is left to the end.

Ciceronian suspended structure can be created in English, especially through the repetition of introductory subordinate clauses:

But the pursuit of truth, when it is profound and genuine, requires also a kind of humility which has some affinity to submission to the will of God. The universe is what it is, not what I choose that it should be. If it is indifferent to human desires, as it seems to be; if human life is a passing episode, hardly noticeable in the vastness of cosmic processes; if there is no superhuman purpose, and no hope of ultimate salvation, it is better to know and acknowledge this truth than to endeavor, in futile self-assertion, to order the universe to be what we find comfortable.

Bertrand Russell, "The Value of Free Thought," in
Understanding History, 102

Here a conditional sentence is elaborated to the left of the main verb, by the multiplication of introductory clauses. This is a true Ciceronian structure, as in the passage quoted at the beginning of this chapter. The next passage has a similar structure of introductory conditional clauses, though the conditional word "if" is used only once:

> If we do not feel at times that the hero is, in some sense, a doomed man, that he and others drift struggling to destruction like helpless creatures borne on an irresistible flood towards a cataract; that, faulty as they may be, their fault is far from being the sole or sufficient cause of all they suffer; and that the power from which they cannot escape is relentless and immovable, we have failed to receive an essential part of the full tragic effect.

> A.C. Bradley, *Shakespearean Tragedy*, Lecture I, 4.

Broken into its components, the sentence looks like this:

> If we do not feel at times
> (1) that the hero is, in some sense, a doomed man,
> (2) that he and others drift struggling to destruction like helpless creatures borne on an irresistible flood towards a cataract;
> (3) that, faulty as they may be, their fault is far from being the sole or sufficient cause of all they suffer; and
> (4) that the power from which they cannot escape is relentless and immovable, we have failed to receive an essential part of the full tragic effect.

The examples from Russell and Bradley are conditional sentences, but other kinds of introductory subordinate clauses can also be multiplied. In the following passage, Bruno Bettelheim explains the value of fairy tales in the psychological development of a child:

> When all the child's wishful thinking gets embodied in a good fairy; all his destructive wishes in an evil witch; all his fears in a voracious wolf; all the demands of his conscience in a wise man encountered on an adventure; all his jealous anger in some animal that pecks out

the eyes of his archrivals—then the child can finally begin to sort out his contradictory tendencies.

Bruno Bettelheim, *The Uses of Enchantment*, 66

Here the temporal conjunction "when"—which goes with each of the introductory subordinate clauses—takes the place of "if," but the force of the sentence is still conditional. In the next passage the introductory word is "where," in four successive adjective clauses:

In the loveliest town of all, where the houses were white and high and the elm trees were green and higher than the houses, where the front yards were wide and pleasant and the back yards were busy and worth finding out about, where the streets sloped down to the stream and the stream flowed quietly under the bridge, where the lawns ended in orchards and the orchards ended in fields and the fields ended in pastures and the pastures climbed the hill and disappeared over the top toward the wonderful wide sky, in this loveliest of all towns Stuart stopped to get a drink of sarsaparilla.

E.B. White, *Stuart Little*, 100

The periodic suspension is only part of the beauty of this passage. In addition White gives us two sets of parallels with increasing numbers:

(1) where
the houses were white and high and
the elm trees were green and higher than the houses,
(2) where
the front yards were wide and pleasant and
the back yards were busy and worth finding out about,

and then two sets of gradatio, again ending with the longest phrase:

(3) where
the streets sloped down to the stream and
the stream flowed quietly under the bridge,
(4) where

the lawns ended in orchards and
the orchards ended in fields and
the fields ended in pastures and
the pastures climbed the hill and disappeared over the top toward
the wonderful wide sky,

After this long rhetorical flourish, the beginning is recapitulated:

in this loveliest of all towns

And the final clause contains the subject, the main verb, and a most euphonious object:

Stuart stopped to get a drink of sarsaparilla.

It is often said that dissection kills beauty, but I think that analysis only increases my admiration for this passage. The effect may not be Ciceronian, but White uses the tools of classical rhetoric with grace and subtlety.

The next passage is even more complex. After two short exclamatory clauses, Defoe continues with a series of antitheses, followed by a series of nested subordinate clauses:

How strange a chequer-work of Providence is the life of man! and by what secret differing springs are the affections hurried about as differing circumstances present! To day we love what to morrow we hate; to day we seek what to morrow we shun; to day we desire what to morrow we fear; nay, even tremble at the apprehensions of. This was exemplify'ed in me, at this time, in the most lively manner imaginable; for I, whose only affliction was, that I seemed banished from human society, that I was alone, circumscribed by the boundless ocean, cut off from mankind, and condemned to what I called silent life; that I was as one whom Heaven thought not worthy to be numbered among the living, or to appear among the rest of His creatures; that to have seen one of my own species would have seemed to me a raising from death to life, and the greatest blessing that Heaven it self, next to the supreme blessing of salvation, could bestow; I say, that I should now tremble at the very apprehensions of seeing a man, and was ready to sink into the ground at but the shadow or silent appearance of a man's having set his foot in the island.

Daniel Defoe, *Robinson Crusoe*, 164

Although Defoe is not usually considered much of a stylist,[6] this passage is neither simple nor artless.

The next passage illustrates a further complication. Here David Knowles is drawing a contrast between Plato and Aristotle; after an introductory sentence, he presents one long period about Plato, and then another long period about Aristotle. The complication lies in the elaboration of the subjects through multiple adjectival prepositional phrases:

The characteristic elements of the two may be juxtaposed; they cannot be fused. To many, Plato, with his exquisite style, perhaps the most flexible and melodious vehicle of thought the world has ever known— Plato, with his unforgettable picture of Socrates, with his deep moral earnestness and lofty idealism, with his unshakeable faith in the beautiful and in the good, with his vision of the godlike soul and its immortal destiny, with his soaring flight from what is temporal and visible to what is unseen and eternal—to many Plato will always seem to mirror so faithfully all the nobler intuitions of the human mind that his supremacy will remain unassailable and even unchallenged. Yet to others the majestic fabric of Aristotle's thought, massive even when shorn of the vast substructure of biology and physics—Aristotle, with his cool and limpid sanity, with his knowledge, which never becomes cynical, of the common man, with his inspired common sense and the sudden vistas that he opens upon the steep-down gulfs of metaphysics—Aristotle, with his insistence upon the value of observation and action in the visible world, with his unwavering assertion that our powers and faculties can of their nature attain to truth and reality each in its own sphere and measure, with his unrivalled precision of terminology and his sureness of touch in analysis and combination—to many Aristotle will seem to have reached the limits of the human mind's achievement here below. That immortal rivalry, overt or unperceived, will vex the greatest minds throughout the middle ages.

David Knowles, *The Evolution of Medieval Thought*, 4–5

The syntax is not entirely parallel; in the third sentence, the subject at first seems to be "the majestic fabric of Aristotle's thought," but then it settles down to just "Aristotle." Although a critical grammarian might be concerned about this structural uncertainty, surely the sense is clear. In long periods such as these, we often find the writer restating the subject to make the ending of the sentence clear; Defoe marks the resumption with the phrase "I say," while Knowles simply repeats "to many Plato" and "to many Aristotle."

Although Cicero has become most celebrated for his long periods, he was equally skilled in the construction of short clauses, and he mixes the short and the long with great care. His style is never monotonous. In the next passage, R.H.Tawney shows some concern for variation in rhythm:

> Rightly or wrongly, with wisdom or with its opposite, not only in England but on the Continent and in America, not only in one denomination but among Roman Catholics, Anglicans, and non-conformists, an attempt is being made to restate the practical implications of the social ethics of the Christian faith, in a form sufficiently comprehensive to provide a standard by which to judge the collective actions and institutions of mankind, in the sphere both of international politics and of social organization. It is being made today. It has been made in the past. Whether it will result in a new synthesis, whether in the future at some point pushed further into the tough world of practical affairs men will say,
>> here nature first begins
> her farthest verge, and chaos to retire
>> as from her outmost works, a broken foe
> will not be known by this generation.

R.H.Tawney, Religion and the Rise of Capitalism, 18–19

The passage begins with a series of antitheses, increasing in length:

Rightly or wrongly (2 syllables and 2 syllables)
with wisdom or with its opposite (3 syllables and 5 syllables)
not only in England but on the Continent and in America (6 syllables and 11 syllables)
not only in one denomination but among Roman Catholics, Anglicans, and non-conformists (10 syllables and 15 syllables)

The long ending of this first period itself includes an antithesis:

> an attempt is being made to restate the practical implications of the social ethics of the Christian faith, in a form sufficiently comprehensive to provide a standard by which to judge the collective actions and institutions of mankind, in the sphere both of international politics and of social organization.

This long period is followed by two short clauses in antithesis; these could have been combined in a compound sentence with a conjunction, but Tawney evidently felt the need for contrast and emphasis:

> It is being made today. It has been made in the past.

And he finishes with a flourish: another suspended period, enclosing a poetic tag:

> Whether it will result in a new synthesis,
> whether in the future at some point pushed further into the tough
> world of practical affairs
> men will say,
> > here nature first begins
> > her farthest verge, and chaos to retire
> > as from her outmost works, a broken foe
> will not be known by this generation.

Tawney has used all the tricks, and yet the passage is awkward. Although the beginning of the first period is carefully arranged (perhaps too carefully), the ending has little shape or rhythm, and the accumulation of prepositional phrases is particularly unfortunate. Unlike White's rhetoric, which helps to evoke the tranquil scene he is describing, Tawney's rhetoric just seems to get in the way.

Periodic construction has not been common in recent writing. A long sentence in modern style is more likely to resemble a simple list, an accumulation of elements with no very clear grammatical relationship to the sentence as a whole, elements valued not so much for their place in a coherent and progressive argument as for their vividness, their sensory impact—

little scenes in themselves, placed before the reader's eye. A short sentence often follows. In the following passage, describing a fishing trip, two very long sentences are composed almost entirely of independent little scenes:

> Billy jumps up to help. All he can think to do is reach around from behind and help her squeeze the pole tighter in between her breasts until the reel's finally stopped by nothing more than the pressure of her flesh. By this time she's flexed so taut and her breasts look so firm I think she and Billy could both turn loose with their hands and arms and she'd still keep hold of that pole.
>
> This scramble of action holds for a space, a second there on the sea—the men yammering and struggling and cussing and trying to tend their poles while watching the girl; the bleeding, crashing battle between Scanlon and my fish at everybody's feet; the lines all tangled and shooting every which way with the doctor's glasses-on-a-string tangled and dangling from one line ten feet off the back of the boat, fish striking at the flash of the lens, and the girl cussing for all she's worth and looking now at her bare breasts, one white and one smarting red—and George takes his eye off where he's going and runs the boat into that log and kills the engine.
>
> While McMurphy laughs. Rocking farther and farther backward against the cabin top, spreading his laugh out across the water—laughing at the girl, at the guys, at George, at me sucking my bleeding thumb, at the captain back at the pier and the bicycle rider and the service-station guys and the five thousand houses and the Big Nurse and all of it. Because he knows you have to laugh at the things that hurt you just to keep yourself in balance, just to keep the world from running you plumb crazy.

> Ken Kesey, *One Flew Over the Cuckoo's Nest*, 211–12

This style is particularly suited to cataloguing kaleidoscopic impressions:

> The city looked unfamiliar. There was a jumble of modernity; a myriad of women showing their bare calves, and men in vests and pleated pants; an uproar of workers drilling holes in the pavement, knocking down trees to make room for telephone poles, knocking

down telephone poles to make room for buildings, knocking down buildings to plant trees; a blockade of itinerant vendors hawking the wonders of this grindstone, that toasted peanut, this little doll that dances by itself without a single wire or thread, look for yourself, run your hand over it; a whirlwind of garbage dumps, food stands, factories, cars hurtling into carriages and sweat-drawn trolleys, as they called the old horses that hauled the municipal transport; a heavy breathing of crowds, a sound of running, of scurrying this way and that, of impatience and schedules. Esteban felt oppressed by it.

Isabel Allende, *The House of the Spirits*, 83

Traditionally, the long periodic sentences was organized on the basis of (more or less) logical relationships expressed through grammatical relationships. In the associative style, however, the grammatical relationships are minimal or even absent. Such a style is not well suited to tracing the links in a chain of argumentation, but it is highly appropriate to the depiction of less logical states of mind, as in dreams or drunkenness. The next passage, from *Under the Volcano*, is part of Yvonne's dream:

They were the cars at the fair that were whirling around her; no, they were the planets, while the sun stood, burning and spinning and glittering in the centre; here they came again, Mercury, Venus, Earth, Mars, Jupiter, Saturn, Uranus, Neptune, Pluto; but they were not planets, for it was not the merry-go-round at all, but the Ferris Wheel, they were constellations, in the hub of which, like a great cold eye, burned Polaris, and round and round it here they went: Cassiopeia, Cepheus, the Lynx, Ursa Major, Ursa Minor, and the Dragon; yet they were not constellations, but, somehow, myriads of beautiful butterflies, she was sailing into Acapulco harbour through a hurricane of beautiful butterflies, zigzagging overhead and endlessly vanishing astern over the sea, the sea, rough and pure, the long dawn rollers advancing, rising, and crashing down to glide in colorless ellipses over the sand, sinking, sinking, someone was calling her name far away and she remembered, they were in a dark wood, she heard the wind and the rain rushing through the forest and saw the tremors of lightning shuddering through the heavens and the horse—great God, the horse—and would this scene repeat itself endlessly and forever?—the horse, rearing, poised over her, petrified in midair, a statue, somebody was sitting on the statue, it was Yvonne Griffaton, no, it was the statue of Huerta, the drunkard, the murderer, it was the Consul, or it was a mechanical horse on the merry-go-round, the carrousel, but the carrousel had stopped and she was in a ravine down which a million horses were thundering towards her, and she must escape, through the friendly forest to their house, their little home by the sea.

Malcolm Lowry, *Under the Volcano*, 335–6

This sentence of 287 words is followed by another of 268 words. Lowry could easily have used full stops in a few spots, particularly at the beginning, but the decision not to do so was clearly deliberate. Moreover, the central portion of the passage could not be divided, since it never settles down into a fixed syntactic structure. The effect of the sentence depends on the accumulation of images linked through association rather than reason.

Sometimes, as we will see further in the next chapter, a long associative sentence can seem rather like a large bag full of scrap-ends and discarded leftovers, thrown together any old way. But the rejection of logic does not necessarily entail the rejection of order; an associative sentence can be internally organized. In the following passage, from a story by William Faulkner, Rider returns home with his dog after his wife's funeral:

"But Ah needs to eat," he said. "Us bofe needs to eat," he said, moving on though the dog did not follow until he turned and cursed it. "Come on hyar!" he said. "What you skeered of? She lacked you too, same as me," and they mounted the steps and crossed the porch and entered the house—the dusk-filled single room where all those six months were now crammed and crowded into one instant of time until there was no space left for air to breathe, crammed and crowded about the hearth where the fire which was to have lasted to the end of them, before which in the days before he was able to buy the stove he would enter after his four-mile walk from the mill and find her, the shape of her narrow back and haunches squatting, one narrow spread hand shielding her face from the blaze over which the other hand held the skillet, had already fallen into a dry light soilure of dead ashes when the sun rose yesterday—and himself standing there while the last of light died about the strong and indomitable beating of his heart and the deep steady arch and collapse of his chest which walking fast over the rough going of woods and fields had not increased and standing still in the quiet and fading room had not slowed down.

Then the dog left him.

William Faulkner, "Pantaloon in Black,"
from *Go Down Moses*, 139–40

Faulkner begins with Rider's entry; and as we enter with him we discover the layout of the house:

they mounted the steps and crossed the porch and entered the house—the dusk-filled single room

Nor is this just a room; it is a room where two people lived:

where all those six months were now crammed and crowded into one instant of time until there was no space left for air to breathe,

The repetition of a phrase leads to a closer focus:

crammed and crowded about the hearth
where the fire which was to have lasted to the end of them,
before which in the days before he was able to buy the stove he would enter after his four-mile walk from the mill

Now the scene shifts from the objects—the room, the hearth, the stove—to Rider's wife:

and find her,
the shape of her narrow back and haunches squatting,
one narrow spread hand shielding her face from the blaze over which
the other hand held the skillet,

Now back to the fire:

> had already fallen into a dry light soilure of dead ashes when the sun
> rose yesterday —

Rider himself:

> and himself standing there while the last of light died about

and his physical reactions, displayed in two parallel constructions, the second in antithesis:

> the strong and indomitable beating of his heart and
> the deep steady arch and collapse of his chest
>
> which walking fast over the rough going of woods and fields had
> not increased and standing still in the quiet and fading room had not
> slowed down.

Here we should notice not only the careful progressive construction of the
sentence, but the rhythm; in the final antithesis, the first colon demands a
quick reading, while the second lingers, especially with the three accented
syllables at the very end. In the style of a master like Faulkner, all the elements work together.

9

ॐ

EXCESS

How long is a sentence? How long is a piece of string? (This question was my introduction to metaphysics, in grade three.) As long as you want it to be. How many pieces of string does it take to reach the moon? One, if it's long enough. How many sentences does it take to make a novel? (One, if it's long enough?)

Of course there is no rule. A good sentence in English can be as short as two words— "Jesus wept" (John 11:35)—or as long as a hundred or even several hundred:

> If a sociological theory, collected from historical evidence, contradicts the established general laws of human nature; if (to use M. Comte's instances) it implies, in the mass of mankind, any very decided natural bent, either in a good or bad direction; if it supposes the reason, in average human beings, predominates over the desires, or the disinterested desires over the personal, we may know that history has been misinterpreted, and that the theory is false.
>
> J.S. Mill, *Comte*, 85–6

In this sentence of 75 words the progression of ideas is clear because the grammatical structure—in this case a series of conditional clauses—is clear. The conditions (in technical terms, the *protasis*) are set out in three clauses, each beginning with "if," followed by the conclusion (the *apodosis*):

(1) If a sociological theory, collected from historical evidence, contradicts the established general laws of human nature;
(2) if (to use M. Comte's instances) it implies, in the mass of mankind, any very decided natural bent, either in a good or bad direction;

(3) if it supposes the reason, in average human beings, predominates
    over the desires, or the disinterested desires over the personal,
[then] we may know that history has been misinterpreted, and that
the theory is false.

Furthermore, we can see a certain progression in the ideas stated in the
protasis. The first is rather general—a theory should not contradict the
general laws of human nature. The second suggests a specific law of human
nature—there is no decided bent either for good or bad in the mass of
mankind. And the third is still more specific—in average human beings,
reason does not predominate over desire, and disinterested desire does not
predominate over personal desire. Now the sentence can move on to the
conclusion: that a theory which disregards these laws of human nature
must be false.

But not all long sentences are so clear. In the following passage Edmund
Wilson sums up a long description of Hugo Bamman, one of the chief
characters in the novel *I Thought of Daisy*. Hugo comes from a conservative
Republican family; he has served in the First World War; and now he is
member of the Communist party:

And so he [Hugo] walked among us like a human penance for the
shortcomings of a whole class and culture—of the society which, in
America, had paralyzed in his friends and himself half the normal
responses to life; which had sterilized its women with refinements;
which had lived on industrial investments and washed its hands of
the corruption of politics; which had outlawed its men of genius or
intimidated them with taboos; which so strangely had driven his
father to his Adirondack lake and, on the rare and brief occasions
when he returned for a wedding or a funeral, had seemed to Hugo's
eyes to sadden him, as, to the latter's heartiness and wit, the other
members of the family had returned only so much that was energetically arid, so much that was self-confidently timid and so much
that was cheerfully cold; and which had desolated Hugo's own
soul, when, through empty afternoons of boyhood, he had wondered why he seemed so impotent to break the spell of his tutoring
in the morning, his aunt's nap after lunch, the people for tea in the

afternoon and his late luxurious reading in bed, to work on a paper, to ship on a whaler or to live on a ranch in the West; and which had finally inflicted on him the shame of that day when he had found the crippled Arkansan dictating his letter to his wife to a man half-flayed with mustard-gas—the shame of knowing that a fellow sufferer and one who had suffered more than he, had been afraid to ask him to render what was perhaps the only service for which his education had fitted him.

Edmund Wilson, I Thought of Daisy, 59

Why is this sentence so hard to follow? The structure, once you see how it works, is not so difficult. In a way it isn't so very different from the structure of the passage from Mill. First there is a relatively straightforward clause:

And so he walked among us like a human penance for the short-comings of a whole class and culture—

then the idea expressed by the phrase "of a whole class and culture" is restated in other words:

of the society

and now that society is described in a series of adjectival relative clauses. The first four of these clauses are reasonably clear:

[of the society]
(1) which, in America, had paralyzed in his friends and himself half the normal responses to life;
(2) which had sterilized its women with refinements;
(3) which had lived on industrial investments and washed its hands of the corruption of politics;
(4) which had outlawed its men of genius or intimidated them with taboos;

But now things get more complicated:

(5) which so strangely had driven his father to his Adirondack lake

and, on the rare and brief occasions when he returned for a wedding or a funeral, had seemed to Hugo's eyes to sadden him, as, to the latter's heartiness and wit, the other members of the family had returned only so much that was energetically arid, so much that was self-confidently timid and so much that was cheerfully cold;

Here we have moved from the general to the personal. If that were all, there would be no problem; but this fifth clause has become bloated, perhaps under the force of emotion, and the grammatical relationships are becoming difficult to keep track of. Perhaps the reader can see that it is "the society"—that is, "a whole class and culture"—which has driven his father to the Adirondack lake; it is harder to see that it is the same class and culture which "had seemed to Hugo's eyes to sadden him." The father is saddened because when he displays heartiness and wit, the response of other family members is energetically arid, self-confidently timid, and cheerfully cold. Presumably we are still supposed to remember that at the root of both the father's retreat and the family's coldness is the same society whose shortcomings Hugo "walked among us like a human penance for." But so much has happened in clause five that it takes some effort to remember that the antecedent of the next "which" is still "the society":

(6) and which had desolated Hugo's own soul, when, through empty afternoons of boyhood, he had wondered why he seemed so impotent to break the spell of his tutoring in the morning, his aunt's nap after lunch, the people for tea in the afternoon and his late luxurious reading in bed, to work on a paper, to ship on a whaler or to live on a ranch in the West;

It must be the whole class and culture that is responsible for the desolation of the day—the tutoring in the morning, his aunt's nap after lunch, tea in the afternoon, and reading in bed. What is the connection of all this to the string of infinitives that end the item? I suppose the young Hugo wanted to break this spell by working on a paper, shipping on a whaler, or living on a ranch, but found himself somehow unable. A writer doesn't have to explain everything, but Wilson makes the reader work very hard to fill in all the gaps.

(7) and which had finally inflicted on him the shame of that day
     when he had found the crippled Arkansan dictating his letter to
     his wife to a man half-flayed with mustard-gas—the shame of
     knowing that a fellow sufferer and one who had suffered more
     than he, had been afraid to ask him to render what was perhaps
     the only service for which his education had fitted him.

And it is still a whole class and culture that is responsible for the shame
Hugo felt when he realized that the crippled Arkansan didn't like or trust
him enough to dictate a letter to him. And it is for this reason that he walks
among us as a human penance. The problem with this sentence is not so
much the length as the lack of clear control, beginning particularly in the
fifth section, with its subordinate clause within a subordinate clause. There
is just too much going on.

The basic function of a sentence is to say something about something—
as a logician would say, to make a predication. Some sentences have only
one term in the predication ("It's raining"),[1] others have two ("Jesus
wept"), or three ("John kissed Mary") or four ("John gave Mary a kiss";
"They elected Sam president"). Such simple sentences can be linked by
coordinating conjunctions ("John kissed Mary and Mary blushed") or by
subordinating conjunctions, which express various connections—conditional, causal, or temporal ("If they elected Sam president, they made a mistake"). Furthermore, the terms of the predication may be further characterized, by adjectives, adverbs, or equivalent phrases or clauses ("The old
man often gives lovely presents to his many grandchildren"; "Whenever she
can, Mrs. Jones, who lives next door, gives cookies, which she makes herself, to the children who live in the neighborhood"). But these subordinate
elements should not take over from the main predication. If they are really
the point of the sentence, they should not be grammatically subordinated.
The problem with Wilson's sentence is that the main clause—"He walked
among us like a human penance for the shortcomings of a whole class and
culture"—has been overwhelmed by subordinate relative clauses, which
modify the object of a prepositional phrase ("of the society"), which in turn
restates another prepositional phrase ("of a whole class and culture").

That's one way to look at a sentence. But a sentence is not simply the
carrier of information; it is also the expression of an attitude, an emotion, a

view of the world. As such it should not be trammelled by the rules of logic disguised as grammar. The following passage is from an earlier stage in the same description of Hugo. Here the first subject is Hugo's father, but the focus of the passage quickly shifts to Hugo himself. Much of the narrative is hidden in the gaps between clauses; there is a lot of energy here, which perhaps makes it worthwhile to risk confusion:

> He had vowed to stay the winter out in his cabin, but in February he caught a bad cold which developed into pneumonia, and, despite his protests, he had to be removed to a town where he could have medical attention. His sons were telegraphed at their school; and Hugo, blinking at his sudden release from the agonizing life of prep school, where the boys made fun of his ebullient stuttering, his inability to pronounce *r*, his stiff intractable black hair, and his clothes, which were bought for him by an aunt and which always looked too young for him, lifted his goggles from the frozen ground and gazed about him with singular relief at the ice-ponds and white houses of the North; read nervously half a chapter of Meredith; and, at last, heard his father, dying, mingle texts from Isaiah and Ezekiel with anxious queries about the pump at his camp, which he seemed to fear was irremediably frozen, and with the names of his sisters and his wife.

> Edmund Wilson, *I Thought of Daisy*, 16–17

The chronological narrative helps to organize the long second sentence. The order of the final elements, however, is not chronological. It is interesting to consider the effect of a different arrangement: "and, at last, heard his father, dying, mingle texts from Isaiah and Ezekial with the names of his sisters and his wife, and with anxious queries about the pump at his camp, which he seemed to fear was irremediably frozen." This order increases the bathetic tone, but it reduces the pathos of the original version, ending with the names of his sisters and his wife.

Malcolm Lowry often wrote sprawling sentences not unlike the ones just quoted from Edmund Wilson. Again, there is a certain energy to these effusions, but sometimes also a certain lack of control. The following sentence comes from the first chapter of *Under the Volcano*; a year after the main events recounted in the novel, M. Laruelle is reminiscing:

His passion for Yvonne (whether or not she'd even been much good as an actress was beside the point, he'd told her the truth when he said she would have been more than good in any film he made) had brought back to his heart, in a way he could not have explained, the first time that alone, walking over the meadows from Saint Près, the sleepy French village of backwaters and locks and grey disused watermills where he was lodging, he had seen, rising slowly and wonderfully and with boundless beauty above the stubble fields blowing with wildflowers, slowly rising into the sunlight, as centuries before the pilgrims straying over those same fields had watched them rise, the twin spires of Chartres Cathedral.

Malcolm Lowry, Under the Volcano, 12

The parenthesis introduces an irrelevancy and sits oddly with the otherwise elegaic tone of the sentence. Nor is this a solitary example. In the passage that follows, Hugh has been listening to a tune on the radio played by jazz violinist Joe Venuti, who often recorded with guitarist Ed Lang:

Joe Venuti had not been the same, one heard, since Ed Lang died. The latter suggested guitars, and if Hugh ever wrote, as he often threatened to do, his autobiography, though it would have been rather unnecessary, his life being one of those that perhaps lent themselves better to such brief summation in magazines as "So and so is twenty-nine, has been riveter, songwriter, watcher of manholes, stoker, sailor, riding instructor, variety artist, bandsman, bacon-scrubber, saint, clown, soldier (for five minutes), and usher in a spiritualist church, from which it should not always be assumed that far from having acquired through his experiences a wider view of existence, he has a somewhat narrower notion of it than any bank clerk who has never set foot outside Newcastle-under-Lynne"—but if he ever wrote it, Hugh reflected, he would have to admit that a guitar made a pretty important symbol in his life.

He had not played one, and Hugh could play almost any kind of guitar, for five years, and his numerous instruments declined with his books in basements or attics in London or Paris, in Wardour Street nightclubs or behind the bar of the Marquis of Granby or the old

Astoria in Greek Street, long since become a convent and his bill still
unpaid there, in pawnshops in Tithebarn Street or the Tottenham
Court Road, where he imagined them as waiting for a time with all
their sounds and echoes for his heavy step, and then, little by little,
as they gathered dust, and each successive string broke, giving up
hope, each string a hawser to the fading memory of their friend,
snapping off, the highest pitched string always first, snapping with
sharp gun-like reports, or curious agonized whines, or provocative
nocturnal meows, like a nightmare in the soul of George Frederic
Watts, till there was nothing but the blank untumultuous face of the
songless lyre itself, soundless cave for spiders and steamflies, and delicate fretted neck, just as each breaking string had severed Hugh
himself pang by pang from his youth, while the past remained, a tor-
tured shape, dark and palpable and accusing.

Malcolm Lowry, *Under the Volcano*, 154–5

There are several problems in this passage. The beginning of the second
paragraph is awkward: "He had not played one" is negative, but it is followed by the positive "and Hugh could play almost any kind of guitar." Not
until the next phrase is the confusion resolved: "for five years." It might have
been better to rearrange: "Though Hugh could play almost any kind of guitar, he had not played for five years." The rest of this sentence seems to me
overwritten, but the flow of ideas and images is not hard to understand.

The long sentence in the first paragraph, however, needs major revision.
The transition from Venuti to Lang to Hugh is not elegant; although it
could be justified as a chain of associated thoughts, one wonders whose
thoughts they are: Hugh's? or the narrator's? The conditional clause "if
Hugh ever wrote . . . his autobiography" is interrupted by "as he often
threatened to do." This interruption by itself would not be so bad, but the
conclusion of the condition is hopelessly delayed by a concessive clause
filled with superfluous information:

> though it would have been rather unnecessary,
> his life being one of those that perhaps lent themselves better to such
>   brief summation in magazines as
> "So and so is twenty-nine, has been

> riveter, songwriter, watcher of manholes, stoker, sailor, riding instructor,
>   variety artist, bandsman, bacon-scrubber, saint, clown, soldier (for
>   five minutes), and usher in a spiritualist church,
> from which it should not always be assumed that
> far from having acquired through his experiences a wider view of exis-
>   tence,
> he has a somewhat narrower notion of it than any bank clerk who has
>   never set foot outside Newcastle-under-Lynne" —

By this time the reader has likely lost the thread, so the sentence starts over
again:

> but if he ever wrote it, Hugh reflected, he would have to admit that
> a guitar made a pretty important symbol in his life.

If all this information about Hugh's life is important, perhaps it should make
a sentence of its own rather than insinuate itself, like a virus, in a sentence
that has a job of its own to do.

Even a fairly short sentence can be too long if it tries to carry too many
ideas or if the structure is not clear. The key to comprehension, in short sentences as in long ones, is the flow of information.

> This book—the record of a people who have moved faster than any
> people of whom we have records, a people who have moved in fifty
> years from darkest savagery to the twentieth century, men who have
> skipped over thousands of years of history in just the last twenty-five
> years—is offered as food for the imagination of Americans, whom
> the people of Manus so deeply admire.
>
> > Margaret Mead, *New Lives for Old:*
> > *Cultural Transformation—Manus, 1928–1953,* 33

Mead has two main ideas here, one of which is stated inside the dashes, the
other outside. If the idea inside the dashes could be expressed briefly, there
would be no trouble: something like "This book—the record of a people
who have skipped over thousands of years of history in just the last twenty
five years—is offered as food for the imagination of Americans, whom the
people of Manus so deeply admire." As it is, by the time the parenthetical

information has been delivered, the sense of the main clause has been lost. If all the ideas in the original are to be kept, the sentence should be divided, one way or another:

> This book is offered as food for the imagination of Americans, whom the people of Manus so deeply admire. It is the record of a people who have moved faster than any people of whom we have records, a people who have moved in fifty years from darkest savagery to the twentieth century, men who have skipped over thousands of years of history in just the last twenty-five years.

> This book is the record of a people who have moved faster than any people of whom we have records, a people who have moved in fifty years from darkest savagery to the twentieth century, men who have skipped over thousands of years of history in just the last twenty-five years. I offer it as food for the imagination of Americans, whom the people of Manus so deeply admire.

Mead has a habit of interrupting her sentences. Here is another example, from the same page:

> Every mile of my voyages to Manus is relevant to the whole problem of what American civilization—a civilization dedicated to the proposition that all men are created equal, created with a right of equal access to all that men have learned and made and won, a civilization made of men who changed after they were grown—has to give, to Americans and to the people of the world with whom we work.

> Margaret Mead, *New Lives for Old*, 33

Here again Mead wants to present two ideas; first she wants to say that every mile of her voyages was relevant to the problem of what American has to give to the world, and second, she wants to characterize American civilization. By combining the two she obscures the grammar. The clause "what American civilization has to give," which is the object of the preposition "of," is a transformation of the underlying clause "American civilization has to give what," with the interrogative direct object shifted to the front. But the long and complex parenthetical characterization of

American civilization cuts the interrogative object and the subject away from the verb, with the result that the reader may well lose the thread. Rearrangement can help, but at the cost of a considerable shift in emphasis:

> Every mile of my voyages to Manus is relevant to the whole problem of what Americans and the people of the world with whom we work can gain from American civilization—a civilization dedicated to the proposition that all men are created equal, created with a right of equal access to all that men have learned and made and won, a civilization made of men who changed after they were grown.

A fundamental question remains: is the long characterization of American civilization really necessary?

The desire to stuff a little bit too much into a sentence seems to arise mostly in academic or critical writing. Here Susan Sontag is discussing literary interpretation and why it is seen to be necessary. Most of her discussion is clear, but towards the end she can't resist inserting a parenthesis:

> Interpretation thus presupposes a discrepancy between the clear meaning of the text and the demands of (later) readers. It seeks to resolve that discrepancy. The situation is that for some reason a text has become unacceptable; yet it cannot be discarded. Interpretation is a radical strategy for conserving an old text, which is thought too precious to repudiate, by revamping it. The interpreter, without actually erasing or rewriting the text, is altering it. But he can't admit to doing this. He claims to be only making it intelligible, by disclosing its true meaning. However far the interpreters alter the text (another notorious example is the Rabbinic and Christian "spiritual" interpretations of the clearly erotic Song of Songs), they must claim to be reading off a sense which is already there.

> Susan Sontag, *Against Interpretation*, 6

The parenthesis could wait until the main work of the sentence is over; then this extra information would not interrupt and confuse the grammar:

> However far the interpreters alter the text, they must claim to be reading off a sense which is already there. (A notorious example is

the Rabbinic and Christian "spiritual" interpretations of the clearly erotic Song of Songs.)

And here is Leslie Fiedler doing the same thing twice in a single paragraph:

> Certain underground figures of the Thirties, however, writers who in their own period were labeled reactionary or eccentric, who were despised or condemned or simply overlooked, have come to seem to us to represent the abiding achievement of that period, an achievement which necessarily had to be accomplished in secret and to await in secret the collapse of the Cult of Social Consciousness (with its concomitant hostility to all art not *both* ideologically o.k. and properly middlebrow) and the emergence of a new taste. We have been busy rediscovering these novelists over the past decade or so, with the special glow of satisfaction that comes with learning to relish "one of us" born out of our time. Certain Jewish writers, pioneer exploiters of the ghetto milieu and the rhythms of Jewish-American speech (Abraham Cahan's *Rise of David Levinsky* provided an example of the genre as early as 1917 but remained for nearly twenty years an isolated sport among vulgar or ineffectual novels of Jewish "local color"), have seemed to us, in the light of the practice of the Forties and Fifties, especially significant: Henry Roth, Daniel Fuchs, and Nathaniel West.

> Leslie Fiedler, *Waiting for the End,* 36–7

The first sentence could be divided and the first set of parentheses removed:

> Certain underground figures of the Thirties, however, writers who in their own period were labeled reactionary or eccentric, who were despised or condemned or simply overlooked, have come to seem to us to represent the abiding achievement of that period. This achievement necessarily had to be accomplished in secret and to await in secret the collapse of the Cult of Social Consciousness, with its hostility to all art not *both* ideologically o.k. and properly middlebrow, and the emergence of a new taste.

This is not elegant, but at least it is readable (although I am not sure that the achievement of published writers can really be called secret, even if its recognition was delayed.) Perhaps the second sentence of this version could be reordered:

> After the collapse of the Cult of Social Consciousness, with its hostility to all art not *both* ideologically o.k. and properly middlebrow, then a new taste could emerge and the achievement of these writers could be recognized.

Finally, if the second parenthetical comment were moved to the end of the passage, it could stand on its own, without the parentheses:

> Certain Jewish writers, pioneer exploiters of the ghetto milieu and the rhythms of Jewish-American speech, have seemed to us, in the light of the practice of the Forties and Fifties, especially significant: Henry Roth, Daniel Fuchs, and Nathaniel West. Abraham Cahan's *Rise of David Levinsky* provided an example of the genre as early as 1917 but remained for nearly twenty years an isolated sport among vulgar or ineffectual novels of Jewish "local color."

I can imagine that Fiedler might object to such domestication of the raw energy of his style, but his habit of interruption can sometimes kill a good effect:

> [*Call it Sleep*] is an astonishingly beautiful and convincing book; but Roth was never able to write another. Bogged down in the midst of a second try, he seems to have undergone a breakdown from which he emerged only to disappear from public view. He has published two or three stories since, of little consequence, and has contributed an occasional statement to a symposium; and there have been, through the years, accounts of his working at some improbable job: attendant in an insane asylum, teacher of mathematics in a high school, most recently poultry farmer outside some small New England town. But what anguish works behind his near-silence we can only—remembering the terror of the novel with which he began and ended—surmise.
>
> Leslie Fiedler, *Waiting for the End*, 48–9

The ending here is unnecessarily flat: the parenthesis robs the sentence of its rhythm. Reordering is possible: "But if we keep in mind the terror of the novel with which he began and ended, we can only surmise what anguish works behind his near-silence." My own choice, however, would be to leave out the parenthesis entirely: "But what anguish works behind his near-silence we can only surmise."

A paragraph, like a sentence, can be too long if it tries to express too many ideas. But the paragraph is less well defined than the sentence; the rules of grammar mostly stop at the level of the sentence, and larger structures are rarely discussed. Very roughly, all the sentences that make up a paragraph should be clearly related to its topic. Different writers have very different senses of how long a paragraph should generally be; and a complex discussion may require separate paragraphs for various points.

As usual, negative examples may be more helpful than positive ones. The following paragraph seems to have two topics: Ezra Pound's way of playing tennis and his literary discussions with Ford Maddox Hueffer and Yeats:

> Pound was now playing tennis regularly with Hueffer on the court available to the tenants of South Lodge; he would listen to what Hueffer had to say about style in the afternoon and that evening he would use it as a lure to draw out Yeats. In this way he encouraged Yeats towards a new gauntness in his poetry and between the two older men managed also to clarify some of his own ideas about style. By all accounts Pound's tennis was a strange sight to behold, with much extraneous leaping and many oddities but very effective against more conventional opponents.

> Noel Stock, *The Life of Ezra Pound*, 138

It is possible that this paragraph is not clumsy but clever; perhaps Stock is elegantly suggesting that Pound's style of tennis resembled his style of conversation. One would feel more confident in such speculation if Stock had not written similar paragraphs elsewhere for no very obvious point:

> Pound was delighted to discover at the Metropolitan gallery one of the finest Goya's he had ever seen. (Twenty-eight years later in *Guide To Kultur* it was no longer one of the best he knew, but "the best.")

This was probably Goya's oil portrait for Don Sebastian Martinez y Perez (1747–1800), lawyer and patron of art, who was general treasurer of the financial council in Cadiz. In the portrait, which was purchased by the Metropolitan in 1906, Don Sebastian is seated and wears a light blue coat. Towards the end of October, he met Witter Bynner, poet and editor, who earlier seems to have played a part in putting him in touch with Small, Maynard & Company.

Noel Stock, The Life of Ezra Pound, 90–1

The ideas in a paragraph ought to have some relationship, some reason for being together. And in most cases there should also be some connection between paragraphs. Such connections are often clarified by a transitional sentence, phrase, or word—usually placed after the paragraph break, but sometimes before it. If there is no explicit mark of transition, there should be at least the sense of a progression, chronological or intellectual. Further discussion of this topic, however, calls for a new chapter.

🍃

10

THE PARAGRAPH AND BEYOND

So far as I know, there has been very little good discussion of the paragraph as a unit of composition. In the 1920s Herbert Read devoted a chapter[1] to the topic, but he didn't say much, and what he did say was largely negative:

> The paragraph is a device of punctuation. The indentation by which it is marked implies no more than an additional breathing space. Like the other marks of punctuation . . . it may be determined by logical, physical, or rhythmical needs. Logically it may be said to denote the full development of a single idea, and this indeed is the common definition of the paragraph. It is, however, in no way an adequate or helpful definition. A good deal depends on what is meant by an "idea"; it is a vague term. But whether we mean an intellectual notion, or a playful fancy, or indeed any definite concept at all, this definition as such will be found of very little application to the paragraphs we find in literature.

But Read has nothing better to offer.

Among the principles of prose writing set out by Robert Graves and Alan Hodge[2] in the 1940s, a few concern the paragraph:

> The order of ideas in a sentence or paragraph should be such that the reader need not rearrange them in his mind.
> The writer should not, without clear warning, change his standpoint in the course of a sentence or paragraph.
> Except where the writer is being deliberately facetious, all phrases in a sentence, or sentences in a paragraph, should belong to the same vocabulary or level of language.
> The same word should not be so often used in the same sentence or paragraph that it becomes tedious.

These are worthy principles, and Graves and Hodge explain them clearly, but without providing much help towards a general understanding of the paragraph.

More recently Joseph Williams has presented a general concept of paragraph construction. A paragraph, he says, consists of two parts: a short opening statement, which introduces the concepts, topics, or themes that will be developed in the rest of the paragraph; and a longer section in which the writer develops "new ideas against a background of repeated topics and themes." The first section he calls the *issue*, the second the *discussion*. "The discussion typically explains, elaborates, supports, qualifies, argues for what the writer stated in the issue. The issue promises; the discussion delivers." Furthermore, each paragraph should have a sentence that expresses the point of the paragraph.[3] As a teacher of undergraduates I know the value of these principles, but they do not begin to account for what real writers actually do.

There are far too many kinds of good paragraphs to discuss them all in a single chapter. And truly bad paragraphs, of the kind we saw at the end of the last chapter, seem to be rare, so I will not focus on faults. Instead this chapter will look at just a few examples of the many ways a good paragraph or group of paragraphs may be constructed. (Since the topic is larger structures, the passages quoted tend to be rather long.)

The following passage is the very beginning of a hard-boiled crime novel by Dashiell Hammett, first published in 1931:

> Green dice rolled across the green table, struck the rim together, and bounded back. One stopped short holding six white spots in two equal rows uppermost. The other tumbled out to the center of the table and came to rest with a single spot on top.
>
> Ned Beaumont grunted softly—"Uhn!"—and the winners cleared the table of money.
>
> Harry Sloss picked up the dice and rattled them in a pale broad hairy hand. "Shoot two bits." He dropped a twenty-dollar bill and a five-dollar bill on the table.
>
> Ned Beaumont stepped back saying: "Get on him, gamblers, I've got to refuel." He crossed the billiard-room to the door. There he met Walter Ivans coming in. He said, " 'Lo, Walt," and would have gone on, but Ivans caught his elbow as he passed and turned to face him.
>
> Dashiell Hammett, *The Glass Key,* 1

The paragraphs here are very short. The fundamental organizing principle is chronology, and the reader must assume that the sequence of the sentences describes the sequence of events. There are, however, a few words or ideas that connect the sentences and the paragraphs: "dice" and "money" in particular. The point of view is almost entirely external, as if seen through a camera—and the whole passage has the feel of a shooting script. The roll of the dice, for instance, is described as if the narrator, like a camera, had no cultural understanding of the game; interpretation is left to the reader, who knows or can deduce that a roll of seven in craps is not good. But the narrator betrays himself in the last paragraph of the passage: to say that Ned Beaumont "would have gone on" requires an interior knowledge of Beaumont's mind and intentions.

Three of the paragraphs begin with the name of a character— "Ned Beaumont," "Harry Sloss," "Ned Beaumont." The principle seems to be that each character owns the paragraph named after him. As soon as there is a shift in camera angle, there is a new paragraph. This pattern continues as Beaumont goes to borrow some money from his friend Paul Madvig:

Madvig asked: "Why don't you try laying off awhile when you hit one of these sour streaks?"

Ned Beaumont scowled. "That's no good, only spreads it out. [. . . .] Might as well take your punishment and get it over with."

Madvig chuckled and raised his head to say: "If you can stand the guff."

Ned Beaumont drew down the ends of his mouth, the ends of his mustache following them down. "I can stand anything I've got to stand," he said as he moved towards the door.

He had his hand on the door-knob when Madvig said, earnestly: "I guess you can, Ned."

Ned Beaumont turned around and asked, "Can what?"

Madvig transferred his gaze to the window. "Can stand anything," he said.

Ned Beaumont studied Madvig's averted face. The blond man stirred uncomfortably and moved coins in his pocket again. Ned Beaumont made his eyes blank and asked in an utterly puzzled tone: "Who?"

Madvig's face flushed. He rose from the table and took a step towards Ned Beaumont. "You go to hell," he said.

Ned Beaumont laughed.

Madvig grinned sheepishly and wiped his face with a green-bordered handkerchief. "Why haven't you been out to the house?" he asked. "Mom was saying last night she hadn't seen you for a month."

Dashiell Hammett, *The Glass Key*, 3–4

Most of *The Glass Key* follows the same pattern—a succession of short paragraphs, made up of dialogue with some indication of the speakers' physical movements but without any direct statement of their ideas or emotions. There are a few narrative passages:

Ned Beaumont, wearing a hat that did not quite fit him, followed the porter carrying his bags through Grand Central Terminal to a Forty-second Street exit, and thence to a maroon taxicab. He tipped the porter, climbed into the taxicab, gave its driver the name of a hotel off Broadway in the Forties, and settled back lighting a cigar. He chewed the cigar more than he smoked it as the taxicab crawled through theatre-bound traffic towards Broadway.

At Madison Avenue a green taxicab, turning against the light, ran full tilt into Ned Beaumont's maroon one, driving it over against a car that was parked by the curb, hurling him into a corner in a shower of broken glass.

He pulled himself upright and climbed out into the gathering crowd. He was not hurt, he said. He answered a policeman's questions. He found the hat that did not quite fit him and put in on his head. He had his bags transferred to another taxicab, gave the hotel's name to the second driver, and huddled back in a corner, white-faced and shivering, while the ride lasted.

When he had registered at the hotel he asked for his mail and was given two telephone-memorandum slips and two sealed envelopes without postage stamps.

Dashiell Hammett, *The Glass Key*, 27

The paragraphs in this narrative section are only slightly longer than those in the sections of dialogue. In the first paragraph there are three sentences; in the second, just one; in the third, four; and in the last, just one again. There are few subordinate clauses. The sentences are linked by the repetition of nouns ("taxicab," "cigar," "hat," "hotel") rather than by conjunctions or adverbs, such as *also, however, likewise, therefore, next,* or *indeed.* And once again, there is no exposition of interior mental activity. The narrator is still largely a camera.

Raymond Chandler's style is very different:

> It was about eleven o'clock in the morning, mid October, with the sun not shining and a look of hard wet rain in the clearness of the foothills. I was wearing my powder-blue suit, with dark blue shirt, tie and display handkerchief, black brogues, black wool socks with dark blue clocks on them. I was neat, clean, shaved and sober, and I didn't care who knew it. I was everything the well-dressed private detective ought to be. I was calling on four million dollars.
>
> The main hallway of the Sternwood place was two stories high. Over the entrance doors, which would have let in a troop of Indian elephants, there was a broad stained-glass panel showing a knight in dark armor rescuing a lady who was tied to a tree and didn't have any clothes on but some very long and convenient hair. The knight had pushed the visor of his helmet back to be sociable, and he was fiddling with the knots on the ropes that tied the lady to the tree and not getting anywhere. I stood there and thought that if I lived in the house, I would sooner or later have to climb up there and help him. He didn't seem to be really trying.
>
> There were French doors at the back of the hall, beyond them a wide sweep of emerald grass to a white garage, in front of which a slim dark young chauffeur in shiny black leggings was dusting a maroon Packard convertible. Beyond the garage were some decorative trees trimmed as carefully as poodle dogs. Beyond them a large greenhouse with a domed roof. Then more trees and beyond everything the solid, uneven, comfortable line of the foothills.

Raymond Chandler, *The Big Sleep,* 3

Chandler writes in the first person, and part of the pleasure of reading his work is the narrator's tone of voice. Philip Marlowe has a lot to say. Even in this descriptive passage, almost everything is worth a comment of some sort, a comparison, a judgment. These comments lengthen the sentences and the paragraphs. The first paragraph has five sentences; the second, five again; the third, four. There are quite a few subordinate clauses. The length of the sentences is quite varied, ranging from 48 words to 7. The rhythm is carefully considered; in the first paragraph, for example, there is a steady decrease in sentence-length—28 words, 25, 14, 10, and 7—leading to a laconic climax.

The paragraphs are well organized. The first, after setting the time, concentrates on the narrator himself, with five uses of "I." The second describes the main hall of the Sternwood place, and in particular the stained-glass panel. The third situates the mansion in the larger landscape.

As Marlowe is inspecting the hallway, waiting for the butler, a young woman (or, as he says, a girl) enters.

She was twenty or so, small and delicately put together, but she looked durable. She wore pale blue slacks and they looked well on her. She walked as if she were floating. Her hair was a fine tawny wave cut much shorter than the current fashion of pageboy tresses curled in at the bottom. Her eyes were slate-gray, and had almost no expression when they looked at me. She came over near me and smiled with her mouth and she had little sharp predatory teeth, as white as fresh orange pith and as shiny as porcelain. They glistened between her thin too taut lips. Her face lacked color and didn't look too healthy.

"Tall, aren't you?" she said.

"I didn't mean to be."

Her eyes rounded. She was puzzled. She was thinking. I could see, even on that short acquaintance, that thinking was always going to be a bother to her.

"Handsome, too," she said. "And I bet you know it."

I grunted.

"What's your name?"

"Reilly," I said. "Doghouse Reilly."

"That's a funny name." She bit her lip and turned her head a little and looked at me along her eyes. Then she lowered her lashes until they almost cuddled her cheeks and slowly raised them again, like a theatre curtain. I was to get to know that trick. That was supposed to make me roll over on my back with all four paws in the air.

"Are you a prizefighter?" she asked, when I didn't.

Raymond Chandler, *The Big Sleep*, 4

Whereas Hammett tended to repeat the name of each speaker in each paragraph of dialogue, Chandler, like most writers, is content to use pronouns or nothing at all. He also divides the dialogue, not just with descriptions of movement, but with commentary, interpretation, and judgment. Although these two writers are generally considered to belong to the same school of hard-boiled detective writers, their styles, and their paragraphs, could not be more different.

Although the form of the narrative may seem simply to imitate the form of the events recounted, of course writing is never so simple. In the first place, most of the events in any work of fiction are invented, so that the form of the narration creates the form of the events, rather than the other way around. Furthermore, in any narration, fiction or non-fiction, there is much that could be told but is left out; a large part of the writer's job is to make a selection among all the events, objects, thoughts, or emotions that could be included. And this selection will to some extent determine the form of the narration.

In any style, from the most laconic to the most loquacious, the coherence of the form will be aided by repetition of key words or ideas. Repetition may occur within a sentence, or it may link sentences and paragraphs. In any case, repetitions are markers that help readers to interpret the story as they read. In the first passage from *The Glass Key* quoted above, the repeated words "dice" and "money" give the passage form and coherence. In the third passage quoted from *The Glass Key*, the repeated elements are "taxicab," "cigar," "hat," and "hotel."

The following excerpt, from the beginning of Frank McCourt's memoir *Angela's Ashes*, is also marked by repetition—and a host of other rhetorical devices:

My father and mother should have stayed in New York where they met and married and where I was born. Instead, they returned to Ireland when I was four, my brother, Malachy, three, the twins, Oliver and Eugene, barely one, and my sister, Margaret, dead and gone.

When I look back on my childhood I wonder how I survived at all. It was, of course, a miserable childhood: the happy childhood is hardly worth your while. Worse than the ordinary miserable childhood is the miserable Irish childhood, and worse yet is the miserable Irish Catholic childhood.

People everywhere brag and whimper about the woes of their early years, but nothing can compare with the Irish version: the poverty; the shiftless loquacious alcoholic father; the pious defeated mother moaning by the fire; pompous priests, bullying schoolmasters; the English and the terrible things they did to us for eight hundred long years.

Above all—we were wet.

Frank McCourt, *Angela's Ashes,* 11

The first paragraph introduces a contrast between New York and Ireland, and the rest of the passage then develops the Irish theme. Also in this first paragraph the theme of childhood is introduced, as the ages of the children are carefully recorded in descending order, ending with the suggestion that to be dead is somehow to be youngest of all.

The second paragraph develops in a general way the combined themes of childhood and Ireland, with great rhetorical flourish, and the third, equally ornate, becomes more specific in its complaints. Then, abruptly, the fourth paragraph introduces a new idea, which is developed in the paragraphs that follow:

Out in the Atlantic Ocean great sheets of rain gathered to drift slowly up the River Shannon and settle forever in Limerick. The rain dampened the city from the Feast of Circumcision to New Year's Eve. It created a cacophony of hacking coughs, bronchial rattles, asthmatic wheezes, consumptive croaks. It turned noses into fountains, lungs into bacterial sponges. It provoked cures galore: to ease the catarrh you boiled onions in milk blackened with pepper; for the congested passages you made a paste of boiled flour and nettles, wrapped in a rag, and slapped it, sizzling, on the chest.

From October to April the walls of Limerick glistened with the damp. Clothes never dried: tweed and woolen coats housed living things, sometimes sprouted mysterious vegetation. In pubs, steam rose from damp bodies and garments to be inhaled with cigarette and pipe smoke laced with the stale fumes of spilled stout and whiskey and tinged with the odor of piss wafting in from the outdoor jakes where many a man puked up his week's wages.

The rain drove us into the church—our refuge, our strength, our only dry place. At Mass, Benediction, novenas, we huddled in great damp clumps, dozing through priest drone, while steam rose again from our clothes to mingle with the sweetness of incense, flowers and candles.

Limerick gained a reputation for piety, but we knew it was only the rain.

Frank McCourt, Angela's Ashes, 11–12

There is much to be said about the rhetoric of this passage—alliteration, asyndeton, metaphor, rhythm—but here I will merely note the unifying theme of water (and other liquids), expressed variously in words like "wet," "rain," "damp" and related terms such as "fountains," "sponges," "steam," and so on. Water moves the story from the ocean, up the river, into the city, into the houses, the pubs, and the churches. Water becomes the fluids of disease, and then their cure. The kingdom of the solid is invaded by the damp, and even human bodies are seen as sluiceways. The behavior and finally the spirit of the people is controlled by water. It is the repetition of words that develops the theme of the passage and gives it coherence.

The above passages from Hammett, Chandler, and McCourt are all narrative (the first two fiction, the third a memoir), but verbal and semantic repetition is perhaps even more important in expository prose. Following is a passage from a recent work of philosophy, Alasdair MacIntyre's *After Virtue*; this is the beginning of the second chapter, entitled "The Nature of Moral Disagreement Today and the Claims of Emotivism":

The most striking feature of contemporary moral utterance is that so much of it is used to express disagreements, and the most striking feature of the debates in which these disagreements are expressed is their interminable character. I do not mean by this just that such debates go on and on and on—although they do—but also that they apparently can find no terminus. There seems to be no rational way of securing moral agreement in our culture. Consider three examples of just such contemporary moral debate framed in terms of characteristic and well-known rival moral arguments. . . .

Alasdair MacIntyre, After Virtue, 6

Although the ideas he is presenting are fairly complex, MacIntyre assists his readers by repeating the key terms— "moral," "contemporary," "disagreement" and "agreement," "debate"—and underlining the relationship between two others: "interminable" and "terminus." These repeated terms are links holding the chain of argument together.

MacIntyre continues with three examples of moral disagreement, concerning war, abortion, and access to essential services through public funding; in each case, he outlines competing and incompatible positions. He then continues:

These arguments have only to be stated to be recognized as being widely influential in our society. They have of course their articulate expert spokesmen: Herman Kahn and the Pope, Che Guevara and Milton Friedman are among the authors who have produced variant versions of them. But it is their appearance in newspaper editorials and high-school debates, on radio talk shows and letters to congressmen, in bars, barracks and boardrooms, it is their typicality that makes them important examples here. What salient characteristics do these debates and disagreements share?

Alasdair MacIntyre, After Virtue, 7–8

This second paragraph is linked to the first by the word "arguments" and also by the phrase "our society," which is a near synonym for "our culture." MacIntyre then adds new information (with something of a rhetorical flourish): although these arguments have "articulate expert spokesmen," what is important about them is their typicality. He ends the paragraph with repetition of "debates" and "disagreements." The next paragraph picks up these links and adds more key terms:

> They [the characteristics of these debates and disagreements] are of three kinds. The first is what I shall call, adapting an expression from the philosophy of science, the conceptual incommensurability of the rival arguments in each of the three debates. Every one of the arguments is logically valid or can be easily expanded so as to be made so; the conclusions do indeed follow from the premises. But the rival premises are such that we possess no rational way of weighing the claims of one as against another. For each premise employs some quite different normative or evaluative concept from the others, so that the claims made upon us are of quite different kinds. In the first argument, for example, premises which invoke justice and innocence are at odds with premises which invoke success and survival; in the second, premises which invoke rights are at odds with those which invoke universalisability; in the third it is the claim of equality that is matched against that of liberty. It is precisely because there is in our society no established way of deciding between these claims that moral argument appears to be necessarily interminable. From our rival conclusions we can argue back to our rival premises; but when we do arrive at our premises argument ceases and the invocation of one premise against another becomes a matter of pure assertion and counter-assertion. Hence perhaps the slightly shrill tone of so much moral debate.

> Alasdair MacIntyre, *After Virtue*, 8

In this paragraph some existing links are repeated ("argument," "debate," "our society," "interminable") while other new links are introduced ("rival," "conclusions," "premises"). And if we were to examine the next paragraph, we would find repetition of the "assertion and counter-assertion" and "shrill."

This may be the first time anyone has compared the styles of Dashiell Hammett and Alasdair MacIntyre, but it is surely interesting to note that these two very different writers share at least one stylistic technique: the use of repeated words and ideas to form links within a paragraph and from one paragraph to the next. Writers who want readers to follow their story or to follow their argument, to see their world or to see their point, will give them as much help as possible.

Repetition is useful at higher levels of formal construction as well. Often the boundaries of a digression will be marked by a repetition. In the following passage Eleanor Harding is going to visit Mary Bold; Eleanor is in love with Mary's brother John, but John has taken a position on church reform that conflicts with the interests of Eleanor's father (the Jupiter, mentioned at the end of the first paragraph, is a newspaper):

> She [Eleanor] put on her bonnet as desired, and went up to Mary Bold; this was now her daily haunt, for John Bold was up in London among lawyers and church reformers, diving deep into other questions than that of the wardenship of Barchester—supplying information to one member of parliament, and dining with another; subscribing to funds for the abolition of clerical incomes, and seconding at that great national meeting at the Crown and Anchor a resolution to the effect that no clergyman of the Church of England, be he who he might, should have more than a thousand a year, and none less than two hundred and fifty. His speech on this occasion was short, for fifteen had to speak, and the room was hired for two hours only, at the expiration of which the Quakers and Mr. Cobden were to make use of it for an appeal to the public in aid of the Emperor of Russia; but it was sharp and effective: at least he was told so by a companion with whom he now lived much, and on whom he greatly depended—one Tom Towers, a very leading genius, and supposed to have high employment on the staff of the Jupiter.
>
> So Eleanor, as was now her wont, went up to Mary Bold, and Mary listened kindly while the daughter spoke much of her father, and perhaps kinder still, found a listener in Eleanor while she spoke about her brother.
>
> Anthony Trollope, *The Warden*, Chapter 10

Since the description of John Bold's activities in London fills in the details of his activities against the interests of Eleanor's father, it certainly has a place in the story. If the digression had been short, no repetition would have been needed:

> She put on her bonnet as desired, and went up to Mary Bold; this was now her daily haunt, for John Bold was up in London among lawyers and church reformers. And Mary listened kindly while the daughter spoke much of her father, and perhaps kinder still, found a listener in Eleanor while she spoke about her brother.

After a long digression, though, readers need to be reminded of where the story left off, and repetition works well as a signpost. This sort of resumptive repetition often comes in the form of dialogue:

> "Well, Julia, is your mamma out?" Anna asked, one Sunday summer afternoon, as she came into the Lehntman house.
>
> Anna looked very well this day. She was always careful in her dress and sparing of new clothes. She made herself always fulfill her own ideal of how a girl should look when she took her Sundays out. Anna knew so well the kind of ugliness appropriate to each rank in life.
>
> It was interesting to see how when she bought things for Miss Wadsmith and later for her cherished Miss Mathilda and always entirely from her own taste and often as cheaply as she bought things for her friends or for herself, that on the one hand she chose the things having the right air for a member of the upper class, and for the others always the things having the awkward ugliness that we call Dutch. She knew the best thing in each kind, and she never in the course of her strong life compromised her sense of what was the right thing for a girl to wear.
>
> On this bright summer Sunday afternoon she came to the Lehntmans', much dressed up in her new, brick red, silk waist trimmed with broad black beaded braid, a dark cloth skirt and a new stiff, shiny, black straw hat, trimmed with colored ribbons and a bird. She had on new gloves, and a feather boa around her neck.
>
> Her spare, thin, awkward body and her worn, pale yellow face though lit up now with the pleasant summer sun made a queer discord with the brightness of her clothes.

> She came to the Lehntman house, where she had not been for several days, and opening the door that is always left unlatched in the houses of the lower middle class in the pleasant cities of the South, she found Julia in the family sitting-room alone.
>
> "Well, Julia, where is your mamma?" Anna asked.

Gertrude Stein, "The Good Anna," Three Lives, 40–1

Umberto Eco uses the same technique in *The Name of the Rose*; Jorge is the blind keeper of the scriptorium of the monastery:

> "The library is testimony to truth and to error," a voice then said behind us. It was Jorge.

The narrator now continues with about 450 words describing Jorge's uncanny ability to know what is going on about him, and his complete knowledge of the library's contents, despite his blindness; and then the story resumes with a repetition designed to bring reader back from the digression:

> "The library is testimony to truth and to error," Jorge said.

Umberto Eco, The Name of the Rose, 129–30

Repetition can also mark large units of composition. Anthony Burgess' *A Clockwork Orange* begins with what looks like a resumptive repetition of the sort we have just been examining. The story takes place in England at some time in the future (or at least future to the date of publication, which was 1962). The narrator of the story, Alex, is a teen-aged hoodlum with equal passions for violence and classical music. The teenagers of the time speak a slang partly derived from Russian, and this is the language in which Alex tells his story. The book begins as he is addressing his friends, or droogs:

> "What's it going to be then, eh?"
>
> There was me, that is Alex, and my three droogs, that is Pete, Georgie, and Dim, Dim being really dim, and we sat in the Korova Milkbar making up our rassodocks [minds] what to do with the evening, a flip dark chill winter bastard though dry.

Anthony Burgess, A Clockwork Orange, 1

Alex then explains that a milkbar sells milk with various legal drugs mixed in. He explains that he and his friends have some money, so they don't really need to mug anyone or rob a shop. He tells what sort of clothes they were wearing, including boots good for kicking people. By now we are on the second page, and the first line of the story is repeated:

"What's it going to be then, eh?"

Alex then explains that there are three girls in the milkbar; but there are four in his group. Alex is tempted to dump Dim, but that would not have been fair. By now we are on the third page:

"What's it going to be then, eh?"

The fellow sitting next to Alex is tripping, and Alex explains what a trip feels like; but he has decided that taking hallucinogens is cowardly. Now we are on page four:

"What's it going to be then, eh?"

By this time the drugs in their milk (perhaps amphetamines) are taking effect, and Alex yells to his droogs, "Out out out out!," and hits the fellow next to him, who doesn't notice. Then Georgie asks "Where out?," and the action begins.

The phrase "What's it going to be then, eh?" seems to be a resumptive repetition of the sort we have seen in "The Good Anna" and *The Name of the Rose*, merely repeated a few more times, to mark the different topics in the long digression. But then Part Two of the book begins with the same phrase:

"What's it going to be then, eh?"
I take it up now, and this is the real weepy and like tragic part of the story beginning, my brothers and only friends, in Staja (State Jail, that is) Number 84F.

Anthony Burgess, *A Clockwork Orange*, 75

Alex has been betrayed by his droogs during a robbery in which an old lady died; he is arrested and convicted of murder and sent to prison. Alex explains exactly how he ended up in prison in a long paragraph that ends, "so that coming and going I was 6655321 and not your little droog Alex not no longer." And then on page 76:

"What's it going to be then, eh?"

Now Alex tells what it has been like to be in prison. By now we are on page 77:

"What's it going to be then, eh?"

And now he explains what is going on at the moment:

I was in the Wing Chapel, it being Sunday morning, and the prison charlie [chaplain] was govoreeting [speaking] the Word of the Lord.

And after another paragraph of scene setting, still on page 77:

"What's it going to be then, eh?" said the prison charlie for the third raz [time]. "Is it going to be in and out and in and out of institutions like this, though more in than out for most of you, or are you going to attend to the Divine Word and realize the punishments that await the unrepentant sinner in the next world, as well as in this?"

So these repetitions are not quite like those at the beginning of Part One. There, the text repeated what Alex said only once, in the sort of resumptive repetition we found in "The Good Anna" and *The Name of the Rose*. Here, the prison charlie repeats his question for emphasis. And these repetitions are not just the prison charlie's; because they repeat the phrase already repeated at the beginning of Part One, they are also the narrator's. In this way they serve to signal not only that a new section of the story has begun, but that in this story form is more important than verisimilitude.

In this second section Alex is subjected to a form of brainwashing; as a result, violence in any form makes him violently ill. Now he is released from prison. Part Three begins on page 130:

"What's it going to be then, eh?"
    That, my brothers, was me asking myself the next morning. . . .

So Alex is out of prison, with just his clothes and a bit of money.

"What's it going to be then, eh?"

He goes to have breakfast in a cheap diner, and then again:

"What's it going to be then, eh?"
What it was going to be now, brothers, was homeways and a nice surprise for dada and mum. . . .

Clearly, then, the overall form of the narrative is in part constituted by these repetitions. But other repetitions are even more fundamental to the shape of the story. The book is divided into three parts: Part One unfolds over a few days just before Alex's arrest, Part Two covers his brainwashing, and Part Three takes place after his release. And every important event of Part One is somehow repeated in Part Three. Thus Part One begins in the milkbar; Alex returns to the milkbar in Part Three. In Part One, after Alex and his droogs leave the milkbar, they attack a harmless fellow who has just left the town library; in Part Three Alex visits the library to find a book that will explain how he can kill himself; there he meets the fellow he attacked, and this fellow and his friends nearly kill him. And so on.

One repeated situation in particular is crucial. In Part One, Alex and his droogs steal a car and drive out to the country, where they find a little cottage. Alex knocks on the door and asks for help. The house is owned by a couple; the husband is a writer, and in fact he is writing a book titled *A Clockwork Orange*. Alex and his friends proceed to beat the man and rape the woman.

Then in Part Three, after Alex has been beaten in the library, the police take him out to the country, where they in turn beat him and leave him stranded. He walks until he finds a cottage, the same cottage he found in Part One. Again he knocks and asks for help. The crisis of the plot develops from this repetition.

11

THE MORPHOLOGY OF THE NOVEL

The novel is notorious as the art-form without a form. It would be easy to gather testimonials to this truism, but one is enough to make the point. E.M. Forster, in his excellent study of the novel, refused to define it precisely:

> Any fictitious prose work over 50,000 words will be a novel for the purposes of these lectures, and if this seems to you unphilosophic will you think of an alternative definition, which will include *The Pilgrim's Progress, Marius the Epicurean, The Adventures of a Younger Son, The Magic Flute, The Journal of the Plague, Zuleika Dobson, Rasselas, Ulysses,* and *Green Mansions*, or else will give reasons for their exclusion? Parts of our spongy tract seem more fictitious than other parts, it is true: near the middle, on a tump of grass, stand Miss Austen with the figure of Emma by her side, and Thackeray holding up Esmond. But no intelligent remark known to me will define the tract as a whole.[1]

Forster's view of definition here is unnecessarily rigid; very few interesting concepts could meet such a standard. And despite his protestations, in fact he offers a fine definition of the novel according to what is now called prototype theory: the works of Austen and Thackeray are prototypes, good central examples of the category designated by the term "novel," even though the edges of the category may be fuzzy.[2]

Later in the same lecture, Forster asked:

> How then are we to attack the novel—that spongy tract, those fictions in prose of a certain extent which extend so indeterminately? Not with any elaborate apparatus. Principles and systems may suit other forms of art, but they cannot be applicable here—or if applied their results must be subject to re-examination. And who is the re-examiner? Well, I am afraid it will be the human heart, it will be this

man-to-man business, justly suspect in its cruder forms. The final test of a novel will be our affection for it, as it is the test of our friends, and of anything else which we cannot define.

Here Forster becomes a bit slippery. He begins with a definite and forceful statement, that the elaborate critical apparatus of principles and systems is not applicable to the novel. But then he backs off and insists only that whatever findings that critical apparatus may produce should be re-examined by the human heart. Could anyone disagree? Consider, for example, an art-form pretty clearly based on an elaborate apparatus of principles and systems—the fugue. Any musicologist knows it is all too possible to write a fugue that is technically correct but has no great artistic value. Here too, the ultimate arbiter is the human heart. The elaborate apparatus is a way to reach the heart, and neither a substitute for nor an obstacle to it. Forster's argument, I believe, is less a reasoned position than an antiformalist reflex—and contradicted in his actual practice as an artist and a critic.[3]

Forster delivered his lectures on the novel in 1927. A flurry of theoretical work began in the 1960s, much of it structuralist in manner and method. Then in the 1980s structuralism fell victim to deconstruction and other varieties of poststructuralism. Some of the deconstructionist critique was valid, particularly the questioning of structuralism's aspirations to hard science; but structuralism in itself did have value, and it was unfortunate that some promising projects were left unfinished when the fashion changed. Among them was the theory of the novel, or, as it came to be called, narratology.[4]

Narratology covers many topics, from structure, realism, and point of view to characterization, and the reader's interaction with the text. I will focus on just the first of these, the question of structure, or the shape of the plot. My discussion draws on earlier theories, but I hope there may be something new here as well.

My basic claim is that the novel does have a form—or rather a set of forms. Forster is right to say that there is no single way to characterize the form of a novel; nor is there any single way to characterize the form of a poem, or a piece of music. Nonetheless, it is possible to discuss the form of a sonnet or a sonata. There is no single form of the novel; novels come in various forms, and these forms can be described. Not all novels will fit the system I propose, but a very large percentage will; and some of the ones that don't fit may show themselves in a new light when we try to see why and how they don't.

Since one of the difficulties in describing the form of the novel has been terminological confusion, I will have to introduce some new terms. Of course the term "novel" itself is radically problematic. The category is sometimes too small, sometimes too large, and the definitions are based on a hodgepodge of criteria—historical, semantic, and formal. For the sake of simplicity I will use the term "novel" generally to mean any long narrative, of any period, realistic or not, in prose or in verse, then introduce further distinctions as needed.

According to Aristotle, a story has a beginning, a middle, and an end:

> A beginning is that which does not itself follow anything by causal necessity, but after which something naturally is or comes to be. An end, on the contrary, is that which itself naturally follows some other thing, either by necessity, or as a rule, but has nothing following it. A middle is that which follows something as some other thing follows it.
>
> Aristotle, *The Poetics*, translated by S.H. Butcher, 65

This passage raises more questions than it answers. What constitutes causal necessity in literature? What about prologues and epilogues? How does the middle link the beginning and the ending? What about deviations from chronological order? Still, Aristotle makes a good starting point. I would revise the first sentence of his comment as follows:

> In (almost) every novel, some social, psychological, or material equilibrium is upset by some specific event, which normally occurs at or near the beginning of both the text and the chronology of the events. This upsetting event (which we may call the hypothesis) enables the story to unfold. Only five hypotheses are in common use: Arrival, Departure, Meeting, Need, and Birth.

This statement is only an approximation—many novels have several sections, each with its own hypothesis—but it will do for now. Here are some examples:

Arrival:

Lewis Carroll, *Alice in Wonderland*
John Cheever, *Falconer*
E.E. Cummings, *The Enormous Room*
Aldous Huxley, *Crome Yellow*
Ken Kesey, *One Flew Over the Cuckoo's Nest*
Thomas Mann, *The Magic Mountain*
Emile Zola, *Germinal*

Departure:

Apollonius of Rhodes, *The Argonautica*
John Bunyan, *The Pilgrim's Progress*
Miguel de Cervantes, *Don Quixote*
Herman Melville, *Redburn*
Katherine Anne Porter, *Ship of Fools*
William Makepeace Thackeray, *Vanity Fair*
J.R.R. Tolkien, *The Lord of the Rings*
Mark Twain, *Huckleberry Finn*
Voltaire, *Candide*

Meeting:

Jane Austen, *Pride and Prejudice*
Honoré de Balzac, *Eugenie Grandet*
Willa Cather, *My Mortal Enemy*
E.M. Forster, *A Room with a View*
Thomas Hardy, *Far from the Madding Crowd*
Henry James, *Washington Square*
Horace McCoy, *They Shoot Horses, Don't They?*

Need:

Apollonius of Rhodes, *The Argonautica*
James Branch Cabell, *Jurgen*
William Faulkner, *As I Lay Dying*
H. Rider Haggard, *King Solomon's Mines*
Aldous Huxley, *Time Must Have a Stop*
R.L. Stevenson, *Treasure Island*
J.R.R. Tolkien, *The Lord of the Rings*

Birth:

    John Barth, *Giles Goat-Boy*

    Robertson Davies, *Fifth Business*

    Daniel Defoe, *Moll Flanders*

    Charles Dickens, *Oliver Twist*

    Charles Dickens, *David Copperfield*

    J.P. Donleavy, *The Beastly Beatitudes of Balthazar B.*

    Henry Fielding, *Tom Jones*

    Günter Grass, *The Tin Drum*

    Thomas Mann, *The Confessions of Felix Krull*

Some of these categories may be further divided: for example, some Births are Mysterious (*Tom Jones, Oliver Twist*), while others are merely Remarkable (*David Copperfield, Fifth Business*). As the distinctions become finer, the discussion of form can become more specific, but it is the first cut into basic categories that makes the project possible. A comparison of *Washington Square* and *A Room with a View* (both Meeting plots) will be fruitful in a way that a comparison of *Washington Square* and *Treasure Island* (a Meeting and a Departure) will not. In somewhat the same way, a fugue is more fruitfully compared to another fugue than to a minuet.

The notion of "social, psychological, or material equilibrium" is easier to understand than to define. At the beginning of *One Flew Over the Cuckoo's Nest*, the society of the mental ward is in an equilibrium, which McMurphy's Arrival upsets. The tension that results is not simply equivalent to conflict: in this case, the ward was full of conflict before McMurphy's Arrival, but the situation was static. The hypothesis is the mechanism that releases the static situation into action. In the same way Huck Finn's Departure (or perhaps the Arrival of his father), the Meeting of Lucy and George (in *Room with a View*), Jason's Need to obtain the golden fleece, and the Birth of Tom Jones all upset an equilibrium and launch a story. In short, the hypothesis functions as the authorial *fiat*: let McMurphy arrive on the ward, let Lucy meet George, and so on. (The creative process behind this *fiat*, of course, may begin anywhere at all.)

Some other hypotheses do occur. More than a few novels begin with a death (*Funeral Rites*, by Jean Genet, *A Death in the Family*, by James Agee); and if mysteries are included, Death becomes a fruitful category indeed, though in a somewhat restricted genre. Many medieval epics begin with an insult, as does the *Iliad*. Marriage, in today's society, is becoming a more frequent narrative hypothesis. None of these hypotheses, however, occurs nearly so frequently as the five outlined above. In any case, the structural principles of narration are not changed by the use of another kind of hypothesis.

Some narratives have more than one hypothesis. *Pride and Prejudice*, for example, begins with the Arrival of Mr. Darcy; then he Meets Elizabeth. In this case, the Meeting is probably the more important event, but the Arrival does have a function in the structure of the story. In general, each new section of a compound narrative is likely to have a new hypothesis. The hypothesis is not necessarily the absolute beginning of either the text or the chronology. Many novels open with a description of the equilibrium that the hypothesis will upset. Sometimes the chronology of the story is altered so that the narrative opens with the hypothesis and a retrospect follows, as in *The Magic Mountain* and many other novels.

The second sentence of Aristotle's description I would also recompose:

> At or near the end of both the text and the chronology of events, a new equilibrium may be established by some specific event, which we may call the cadence. Some typical cadences are Departure, Return, Arrival, Marriage, Death, Discovery, and Satisfaction.

There is no necessary correlation between hypothesis and cadence, but some pairings seem natural. Thus many Arrival plots end with a Departure: *The Enormous Room, Falconer, Crome Yellow, Germinal, The Magic Mountain*; but in *One Flew Over the Cuckoo's Nest* the Departure of Chief Broom (and other inmates) is combined with the Death of McMurphy. *Alice in Wonderland* is one of a large and important class of Arrival plots that take place not in a single confined space but in a new a world in which the characters move freely. This form is often found in Utopian fiction, whereas the Arrival to a confined space is typical of what Edwin Muir[5] calls the dramatic novel, which is intense rather than diffuse in effect. In many Arrival narratives, of either type, there is some sense of division between the world on the outside and the world on the inside. If the outside world is shown (as it is in *One Flew Over the Cuckoo's Nest* and *Alice in Wonderland*, but not in *Germinal*), the cadence may be not just a Departure but also a Return.

A Departure plot may end with an Arrival, particularly if some goal is implicit in the hypothesis (*The Pilgrim's Progress*), or with a Return (*Don Quixote, Redburn*; in both of these there is also a Death); but in others the movement has no particular direction (*Vanity Fair*). Though most Departure plots are expansive, if the characters travel in a confined space (on a ship or in a train) the story can become intensive (as in *Moby-Dick* or *Ship of Fools*).

Many Meeting plots end with a Marriage (*Pride and Prejudice, A Room With a View*). The strength of this convention gives additional meaning to Marriage Denied cadences (*Eugenie Grandet, Washington Square*).

Need plots are no longer common in high-culture narrative. However, the Quest (Need plus Departure/Satisfaction plus Return) has been one of the most important elements of narrative since Gilgamesh, and the form is still popular in adventure stories.

Birth plots often end with either Death (*Moll Flanders*) or Marriage (*David Copperfield*). Mysterious Births, of course, are usually resolved with Discovery. *The Tin Drum* ends with the protagonist in a mental hospital; if Thomas Mann had finished *The Confessions of Felix Krull*, the hero would have ended up in jail. *The Beastly Beatitudes of Balthazar B.* ends not with any firm cadence, but with a sense of a completed pattern that is not likely to change.

Some hypotheses strongly determine the course of the story. The reader can confidently expect the typical Meeting hypothesis to end with a Marriage, or the typical Need hypothesis to end with Satisfaction, after the appropriate obstacles have been overcome. But some hypotheses do not predict very much; a Birth or a Departure may require one or more additional hypotheses along the way.

A narrative may end without a cadence, with a simple resolution of conflict or re-establishment of a familiar pattern. A cadence provides a greater sense of an ending, particularly if the cadence matches the hypothesis (Arrival/Departure, Birth/Death, etc.) There may also be a final repetition of some event, situation, or phrasing introduced at the beginning of the story. Events or situations from the chronological end of the story may be brought forward to the beginning of the narrative, artificially producing a final repetition.

The third sentence of Aristotle's account I would also revise:

> The material between the hypothesis and the cadence (which we
> may call the development) will consist of events that either hinder
> or facilitate the movement towards the cadence, along with charac-
> ter analysis, descriptions, digressions, and commentary.

The events of the development section are more variable than those of the
hypothesis and cadence—similarly in sonata form, the development section
is structurally more free than the exposition or the recapitulation.
Nevertheless, analysis of some of the more formalized subgenres will usually reveal some basic patterns. Many adventure stories develop in rather
similar ways, as do many Meeting/Marriage plots where the obstacles are
primarily social or psychological.

A novel, then, is made of chains of events, each beginning with a
hypothesis, proceeding through a development, and ending with a cadence;
a narrative sequence with these three parts we may call a movement. A
novel may consist of a single movement with complex obstacles, or of several movements combined in various ways. Some narratives are simply linear strings of plot movements, one after another (as in *The Canterbury Tales*);
some are linked chains of movements all involving the same characters
(Nabokov's *Pnin*; Updike's *Bech: A Book*); and some linked chains have an
initial hypothesis that receives its cadence only at the end of the whole narrative. Most biographical (Birth/Death) and adventure stories (Departure/
Return) have this form. But movements can be combined in other ways
too: a pair of plots can run more or less side by side, or one plot can be narrated inside another.

The writer's job, like the composer's, is to delay the final cadence. In a
plot with a single movement, the delaying tactics include the introduction
of hindering or facilitating events, detailed characterization, social or psychological analysis, and so on. But even a plot that is fundamentally a single movement may have stages, and these stages will be marked by internal
hypotheses.

It is dangerous to generalize, but I would suggest that Western literature
has seen three stages of long narrative. From Classical times until perhaps as
recently as 1750, most long narratives consisted of several movements in a
chain; single-movement narratives were typically short. By the mid-nine-
teenth century, however, narratives made up of a single complex movement

were becoming common. Since the turn of the twentieth century, many narratives have been written in which the plot is subordinate to other interests. Four characteristics in particular distinguished these new narratives: (1) elaboration of psychological analysis; (2) elaboration of verbal texture; (3) massive alterations of chronology; and (4) an open-ended structure theoretically demanded by the hyper-realist schools of naturalism and impressionism. Although these elements were not entirely absent in earlier periods, only in the past century have they combined to produce a new kind of narrative structure. Even now, however, most narratives, including most high-culture narratives, use the traditional forms outlined in this chapter.

And yet the exceptions deserve some attention as well. These seem to fall into three categories. First, many short stories do not follow the three-part pattern I have outlined. Perhaps they don't need to—perhaps it is only as a story gets longer and more complex that more structure is needed to keep its elements under control and help the reader to stay on track. On the other hand, some very large and sprawling stories are not well analyzed by this scheme: in *War and Peace*, for example, there are numerous Arrivals, Deaths, and Departures, but no single one of them is a fundamental hypothesis. Other novels of this type include Bennett's *The Old Wives' Tale*, García Marquez's *One Hundred Years of Solitude*, and Mann's *Buddenbrooks*.

Second, there is an interesting group of novels in which the narrated time amounts to a single day—*Ulysses*, for example. Most of these novels do not have a regular hypothesis, though some do end with a cadence. In *One Day in the Life of Ivan Denisovich*, Solzhenitsyn portrays a typical day in a Soviet prison camp; the hypothesis/cadence structure would be completely out of place in a work of this sort. In many single-day novels, the day is one of decision, transcendence, or catastrophe; examples include Barth's *The Floating Opera*, Woolf's *Mrs. Dalloway*, and Lowry's *Under the Volcano* (which does seem to have an Arrival hypothesis). Most one-day novels make extensive reference to prior time; in some instances, perhaps, a hypothesis/cadence structure can be found underlying the shifting chronology.

And third, many modernist novels do not follow the three-part pattern. Yet these deviations can be appreciated only if the frameworks from which they deviate are themselves understood. In fact, many modernist writers—among them Gertrude Stein, Samuel Beckett, and William Faulkner—demonstrate profound understanding of the conventions they violate.

All this theory may seem abstract and reductive. Certainly no amount of analysis is a substitute for a real story. It is writers themselves who bring the theory alive, as they use and adapt traditional forms to suit the stories they want to tell. A good example is E.M. Forster in his first novel, *Where Angels Fear to Tread*. Forster may or may not have approached this work with principles and systems in mind, but analysis makes it plain that he knew all the traditional conventions. Here is the opening paragraph:

> They were all at Charing Cross to see Lilia off—Philip, Harriet, Irma, Mrs. Herriton herself. Even Mrs. Theobald, squired by Mr. Kingcroft, had braved the journey from Yorkshire to bid her only daughter goodbye. Miss Abbot was likewise attended by numerous relatives, and the sight of so many people talking at once and saying such different things caused Lilia to break out into ungovernable peals of laughter.

> E.M. Forster, *Where Angels Fear to Tread*, 3

It is clear from the start that the hypothesis of the plot is a Departure. Furthermore, as the reader will soon discover, all (but one) of the important characters are introduced in the first paragraph. Lilia, the only daughter of Mrs. Theobald, is the widow of Charles Herriton. Mrs. Herriton is her mother-in-law, Philip and Harriet are her brother- and sister-in-law, and Irma is her daughter. Mr. Kingcroft is a possible suitor. Miss Abbott has been chosen to be Lilia's traveling companion, to keep her out of trouble. The structure of the paragraph suggests that Lilia is the heroine.

The Herritons are middle-class snobs. Charles married down, and the Herritons, particularly Mrs. Herriton, have expended much energy in trying to improve Lilia, during the marriage and after his death. This trip to Italy is part of her education, as well as a way of keeping her away from Mr. Kingcroft. Philip suggested the trip; he is the relatively unconventional member of the Herriton family, the only one who has traveled in Italy.

The major character in a Departure plot will most naturally be the person who has departed. In this story, however, once Lilia has boarded the train she remains off-stage for the rest of the first chapter. Off-stage, but not out of mind, for the characters left behind—Mrs. Herriton, Philip, and Harriet—do little but talk about her. She writes home often—from

Florence, from Naples, from Rome, and from smaller towns that Philip has recommended. Then they discover that she has become engaged to marry a man she has met in Italy. Worse, her fiancé turns out to be not English, but Italian.

In the second chapter Philip is sent to Italy to rescue Lilia. Yet even now she is not immediately presented to the reader. When Philip gets to Monteriano, the person he speaks to first, and at some length, is Miss Abbott, Lilia's companion. He discovers that he has come too late: Lilia has already married a handsome young fortune hunter named Gino Carella. At the end of the chapter Philip and Miss Abbott return to England, but Lilia stays behind with her new husband.

Forster has used a traditional form—a Departure leading to an Arrival and then a Meeting—but not in the usual way. There are many novels in which the hero or heroine goes to a foreign country and meets someone; at the end of the story the two either marry or for some reason fail to do so. In such stories the meeting is usually presented in careful detail, and the obstacles to the marriage take up the bulk of the book. Henry James offers several examples: *The American*, *The Portrait of a Lady*, *The Ambassadors*. Here, though, the meeting is never presented at all; the character one expects to be the heroine is mostly off-stage; the subsidiary characters are in the spotlight; the obstacle arrives too late; and so the marriage takes place almost at the beginning of the story.

But in another way Forster's use of the form is quite conventional. Very often a Departure/Arrival hypothesis is used to establish a contrast between two cultures—as, for example, in utopian fiction. In this story, Forster represents English middle-class society as civilized, superficial, and repressed; Italy is The Other: natural, spontaneous, vital. One may smile at the stereotypes, but Forster handles them effectively.

 Not until Philip and Miss Abbott have left does Lilia take center-stage. Her marriage is not happy. Gino spends most of his time in the caffès with his friends, but Lilia has no friends and no place in the society of a small Italian town. When she discovers that he has been unfaithful, they fight. Finally, at the very end of Chapter Four, Lilia gives birth to their baby and dies.

Once again Forster has fiddled with the conventions. It is not right for the central character of a novel to die less than half way through. Evidently this story is not to be about Lilia. Who, then, is the central character?

Lilia's Death is the cadence of the first part of the novel, and the Birth of her son is the hypothesis of the second part of the novel. The Herritons are presented with a problem. If Lilia had died childless, they could simply forget about her. But the child in some sense belongs to them, and it would be uncivilized to let him be brought up in savage Italy. Then Caroline Abbott forces a decision. She tells the Herritons that she feels personally responsible for the birth; she, after all, was supposed to keep an eye on Lilia. Once she starts to interfere, the Herritons feel that they have no choice. Mrs. Herriton sends Philip and Harriet to Italy to bring the baby back to England. So the second part of the novel has its own Departure and Arrival, as well as a Birth.

When Philip and Harriet reach Monteriano they are surprised to find that Caroline Abbott is there before them. By now she and Philip have talked several times, and to his surprise he has found that she is not merely a conventional middle-class English woman: she shares many of his objections to the restrictions of their society, and she too seems impressed by the vitality of Italy. Philip is gradually developing an interest in Miss Abbott.

Philip intends to visit Gino the next morning to buy the baby from him, but Miss Abbott gets there first. When she sees Gino with his son, she realizes that he truly loves the baby, and learns that he has arranged to marry again so that the child will have a mother. Philip comes in just as she has given up the idea of taking the child away; she leaves in some distress.

Philip tries to persuade Gino to give up the child, but he fails. A second attempt to negotiate also fails. He and Harriet decide to leave that evening. Miss Abbott has also decided to leave; but since, in Harriet's eyes, Miss Abbott has become a traitor, they cannot leave together. Two carriages are ordered to take them to the station.

That evening, however, as Philip is preparing to leave, Harriet is nowhere to be found. She sends him a note saying that he should start out in the carriage and meet her outside the town. When he arrives he finds that she has gone to Gino's house and stolen the baby. They are on the way to the station when there is an accident; Philip is injured and the baby is killed. (Evidently it was just a prop, as children often are in novels.)

Philip goes to tell Gino that the baby is dead. Gino attacks him, but Miss Abbott arrives and stops the fight. Their emotions apparently purged, Gino and Philip in an odd way become friends.

The last chapter of the novel is taken up with a long conversation between Philip and Miss Abbott. They are on the train, heading home to England. Harriet is in another compartment. During the conversation, Philips realizes that he has fallen in love with Miss Abbott, but just as he is about to declare himself, she reveals that she has fallen in love with Gino. Of course she cannot marry him, since he has already arranged a new marriage, and Philip cannot now marry her. So the novel ends with renunciation.

An outline of the plot in the terms of the system proposed above would look something like this: Part One begins with a Departure, which leads to an Arrival and a Meeting and a Marriage. Part One ends with a Birth and Death. The Birth at the end of Part One becomes the hypothesis of Part Two; this Birth leads to a new Departure and Arrival. Then the Death of the baby leads to a final Departure and a double Marriage Denied cadence. By then, Philip and Miss Abbott have become the principal characters of the story.

Certainly this kind of analysis leaves out much of what is wonderful about the book—Forster's brilliant style, his subtle and cynical psychological analysis. But the structure of the plot is not simply an armature for style and characterization; on the contrary, the arrangement of events, within and against the traditions and conventions of the genre, is an essential part of the story's meaning. Confident that his readers would know the conventions, Forster could use them to create expectations and disappoint them. If the novel were truly an art-form without form, he could not have done so.

I chose to discuss *Where Angels Fear to Tread* because it is a short novel with a complex plot, and because that complexity is clearly part of the story's meaning. When Forster wrote it, did he have those conventions in mind? I suspect that he did; his own criticism shows that he had thought deeply about many aspects of the novel, including plot. But knowledge does not have to be conscious to be effective. Certainly many writers—and many other artists—would find it hard to explain how or why they do what they do. Some might find the very questions absurd; for them, the point is simply to do—analyzing the technicalities is for the critics and teachers.

Stylistic analysis is one thing, the psychology of creation another. No doubt there are writers who would rather not know about the technicalities of style—rhythm, sentence and paragraph structure, figures of speech, the conventions of plot construction—and with these people I have no quarrel. Still, the Romantic conception of the artist as an inspired idiot now looks like a brief aberration. Through most of the history of Western culture writers knew what they were doing, and their art did not suffer from this knowledge. If you are one of those—writers, editors, and readers—who like to know what lies behind the mystery, I hope you have enjoyed this book.

NOTES

INTRODUCTION

1 *Hitler*, vol. 1, *1889-1936: Hubris*; vol. 2, *1936-1945: Nemesis* (New York: Norton, 2000).

1 THE ARRANGEMENT OF WORDS

1 A new translation by Rodney J. Payton and Ulrich Mammitzsch, titled *The Autumn of the Middle Ages* (Chicago: University of Chicago Press; 1996), aims to correct the faults of the original English edition, which was somewhat abridged, but their version of the passage in question (on 232) does not add to our discussion.

2 John Marsh, *The Fullness of Time* (London: Nisbet, 1952). The others mentioned by Kermode are Oscar Cullman, *Christ and Time* (Philadelphia: Westminster Press, 1951); Frank Herbert Brabant, *Time and Eternity in Christian Thought* (London: Longmans, 1937). In the passage, Kermode refers to James T. Barr, *Biblical Words for Time* (London: SCM Press, 1962).

3 For discussion of the question, see "Any and some," Chapter Two of *Meaning and Form*, by Dwight Bolinger (London: Longmans, 1967).

3 RHYTHM

1 There are several good handbooks that treat metrics in some detail; I particularly like *Poetic Meter and Poetic Form*, by Paul Fussell (New York: Random House, 1965, 1979).

2 All of this classical theory of prose rhythm is discussed by L.P. Wilkinson in *Golden Latin Artistry* (1963; Norman: University of Oklahoma Press, 1985), Chapter 5, 135-64.

3 For ease of presentation I mark only the stressed syllables, using an acute accent; feet are divided by a vertical line.

4 For further critique of Saintsbury's method, see D.W. Harding's *Words into Rhythm* (Cambridge: Cambridge University Press, 1985).

5 As Mary Cross says (in *Henry James: The Contingencies of Style,* 1) "Reading Henry James can make us feel as uneasy and disoriented as some of his characters are. In the maze of James's language, both readers and characters find themselves struggling to get their bearings somewhere in his sentences, trying to contain their constant flicker and spill of meaning. James's sentences, indeed, are disorienting, keeping things off balance by their delaying tactics, ambiguity of reference, and proliferating clause and phrase" (*Henry James: The Contingencies of Style* [New York: St. Martin's, 1993]). For other discussions of James's style, see Seymour Chatman, *The Later Style of Henry James* (Oxford: Blackwell, 1972), and Ruth Bernard Yeazell, *Language and Knowledge in the Late Novels of Henry James* (Chicago: University of Chicago Press, 1976).

4 ORNATE STYLE

1 "Current" here means "good money" as opposed to counterfeit.

2 See "The Sources of the Euphuistic Rhetoric," in Morris W. Croll, *Style, Rhetoric, and Rhythm* (1966; Woodbridge, Conn.: Ox Bow Press, 1989).

3 "Brack" here means a flaw in cloth.

4 James Sutherland, *On English Prose* (Toronto: University of Toronto Press, 1957), 77.

5 For discussion of the comic element in Hawkes' writing, see Donald J. Greiner, *Comic Terror: The Novels of John Hawkes* (Memphis, Tenn.: Memphis State University Press, 1973).

6   C.S. Baldwin, *Medieval Rhetoric and Poetic* (Gloucester, Mass.: Peter Smith, 1959), 40.

5 A FEW FIGURES OF SPEECH

1   The study of figures is a part of rhetoric, but rhetoric should not be simply equated with the figures; in the broadest sense rhetoric can include almost all study of the use of language, from the proper construction of an argument to the psychology of the writer and the audience. There are now many good accounts of the history of rhetoric; see, for example, George Kennedy, *The Art of Persuasion in Ancient Greece* (Princeton: Princeton University Press, 1963); also Brian Vickers, *In Defence of Rhetoric* (Oxford: Clarendon Press, 1988).

2   In a related figure, an adjective-plus-noun is turned into two nouns linked by "of," as in "a polish of complexion" for "a polished complexion"; the example is from Henry James, *The Golden Bowl*; Seymour Chatman, in *The Later Style of Henry James* (50–1), notes that this figure is common in James.

3   There is one additional trick; in the fourth line "and [whose] sharp bites she is accustomed to incite," the relative pronoun is omitted; if it were stated, it would be in the genitive, "cuius," thus continuing the polyptoton. This poem is really impossible to translate; the four infinitives "to play" (*ludere*), "to hold" (*tenere*), "to give" (*dare*), and "to incite" (*incitare*) all are dependent on the verb "(she) is accustomed" (*solet*), which is delayed until the fourth line. In English, the main verb must be brought forward, or, as in most of the translations I consulted, left out.

4   *Ada* (London: Weidenfeld and Nicholson, 1969).

5   The literature on metaphor and other kinds of symbolic language is enormous; the following list is only a meager selection. Kenneth Burke's "Four Master Tropes," in *A Grammar of Motives* (Berkeley: University of California Press, 1969), is an influential discussion of metaphor, metonymy, synecdoche, and irony. In *The Philosophy of Rhetoric* (New York: Oxford University Press, 1965), I.A. Richards introduced the terms "vehicle" and "tenor," which have become standard in discussions of metaphor. Christine Brooke-Rose's *A Grammar of Metaphor* (London: Secker and Warburg, 1958) extends the discussion to grammatical structures not usually included under the term. Max Black's two articles "Metaphor," in *Models and Metaphors* (New York: Cornell University Press, 1962), and "More About Metaphor," in A. Ortony, ed., *Metaphor and Thought* (Cambridge: Cambridge Univerity Press, 1979), as well as Eva Feder Kittay's *Metaphor: Its Cognitive Force and Lingustic Structure* (Oxford: Clarendon Press, 1987), examine the figure from a philosophic perspective. George Lakoff and Mark Johnson, in *Metaphors We Live By* (Chicago: University of Chicago Press, 1980) demonstrate the extent of metaphor in everyday language and thought. Perhaps the most comprehensive study is Paul Ricoeur's *The Rule of Metaphor* (Toronto: University of Toronto Press, 1977). And new studies of metaphor appear every year.

6   I take my definitions mostly from Richard A. Lanham's *Handlist of Rhetorical Terms* (Berkeley: University of California Press), the best easily available handbook.

6 MORE FIGURES

1   R. Jakobson, "Poetry of Grammar and Grammar of Poetry," *Lingua* 21 (1968): 597-609; N. Schor, "Fiction as Interpretation / Interpretation as Fiction," in S. Suleiman and I. Crosman, eds., *The Reader in the Text: Essays in Audience and Interpretation* (Princeton: Princeton University Press, 1980); J. Culler, "Structure of Ideology and Ideology of Structure," *New Literary History* 4 (1973): 471-82.

7 PARALLELISM AND ANTITHESIS

1   For discussion and examples of violation of parallelism in Thucydides, see J.S. Rusten's "Introduction" to Thucydides, *The Peloponnesian War*, Book II, 26-7. An excellent analysis of the various types of parallelism and antithesis may be found in W.K. Wimsatt, *The Prose Style of Samuel Johnson* (1941; New Haven: Yale University Press, 1963).

8 PERIODIC SENTENCES

1 The word *phrase* derives from the Greek "phrasis" (φράσις), meaning a speech, a saying, an idiom, an expression, or a phrase.

2 The word *clause* derives from the Latin "clausula," referring to the end of a sentence, and particularly the various rhythms of sentence endings.

3 See George A. Kennedy, "Aristotle on the Period."

4 The word *sententious* used to mean full of meaning, intelligence, or wisdom, but this meaning is now obsolete. Today *sententious* is usually pejorative: a sententious person, a person who relies heavily on maxims, is considered pompous and affected. In *Hamlet*, Polonius is fond of using sentences, and so he is sententious.

5 Fielding punctuates the second and third clauses with full stops, but since they are clearly objects of the verb, we would say that they are part of the same sentence; Fielding's style of punctuation is designed more to guide the reader's voice than to indicate the grammatical structure.

6 Walter Allen, in *The English Novel* (New York: Dutton, 1954), 24, characterizes Defoe as "a man to whom art and literary theory meant nothing"; according to James Sutherland, in *On English Prose* (27), Defoe is among those writers "whose prose has its origin in 'the common intercourse of life,' and because it was never fashionable or learned, has never gone out of style."

9 EXCESS

1 This is a one-place predication because there is no real subject, just a verb. Since English requires an expressed subject, the dummy "it" is inserted. But this pronoun does not stand for a noun: it would make no sense to ask "What's raining?"

10 THE PARAGRAPH AND BEYOND

1 Chapter Five in *English Prose Style* (Boston: Beacon Press, 1952); the passage quoted is on 52.

2 In *The Reader Over Your Shoulder: A Handbook for Writers of English Prose* (1943; New York: Vintage, 1979).

3 *Style: Toward Clarity and Grace* (Chicago: University of Chicago Press, 1990), 92 and 99.

11 THE MORPHOLOGY OF THE NOVEL

1 The two passages quoted are from *Aspects of the Novel* (1927; New York: Harcourt, Brace and World, 1954), 6 and 23.

2 A good discussion of categories and prototype theory may be found in George Lakoff's *Women, Fire and Dangerous Things* (Chicago: University of Chicago Press, 1987).

3 For further anti-formalist discussion of the novel, see Ian Watt, *The Rise of the Novel: Studies in Defoe, Richardson, and Fielding* (1957; Harmondsworth: Penguin, 1983), 14; also George Steiner, *After Babel: Aspects of Language and Translation* (Oxford: Oxford University Press, 1975), 456. These are only two of many possible examples.

4 For a good account of work in narratology, with a good bibliography, see Wallace Martin, *Recent Theories of Narrative* (Ithaca: Cornell University Press, 1986). The theory of plot which I present in this chapter is particularly indebted to Vladimir Propp, *The Morphology of the Folktale* (Bloomington: Indiana University Research Center in Anthropology, Folklore and Linguistics, 1958); Claude Bremond, "The Logic of Narrative Possibilities," *New Literary History* XI, 3 (Spring 1980), 387-411; Thomas G. Pavel, *The Poetics of Plot: The Case of English Renaissance Drama* (Minneapolis: University of Minnesota Press, 1985); and Eugene Dorfman, *The Nareme in the Medieval Romance Epic: An Introduction to Narrative Structures* (Toronto: University of Toronto Press, 1969). See also my article "The Concept of Plot and the Plot of the Iliad," *Phoenix* 55, 1–2 (Spring–Summer 2001), 1–8.

5 In *The Structure of the Novel* (New York: Harcourt, Brace and World, n.d.)

WORKS CITED/CREDITS

Achilles Tatius. *Leucippe and Clitophon*. Translated by S. Gaselee. Cambridge: Harvard University Press, 1969.

Allen, Louis. *Japan: The Years of Triumph*. New York: Library of the 20th Century (American Heritage Press), 1971.

Allen, Walter. *The English Novel*. New York: E.P. Dutton, 1954.

Allende, Isabel. *The House of the Spirits*. New York: Bantam, 1986.

Arendt, Hannah. "Introduction" to *Illuminations*, by Walter Benjamin. New York: Schocken, 1968.

Aristotle. *The Poetics*. Translated by S.H. Butcher. New York: Hill and Wang, 1961.

Austen, Jane. *Emma*, from *The Complete Novels of Jane Austen*. New York: Modern Library, n.d.

———. *Mansfield Park*. Oxford: Oxford University Press, 1975.

———. *Pride and Prejudice*. London: Penguin, 1972.

Baldwin, C.S. *Medieval Rhetoric and Poetic*. Gloucester, MA: Peter Smith, 1959.

Barfield, Owen. *History in English Words*. London: Faber & Faber, 1953.

Barnes, Djuna. *Nightwood*. New York: New Directions, 1961.

Barthes, Roland. *Criticism and Truth*. Minneapolis: University of Minnesota Press, 1987.

Beckett, Samuel. *Watt*. New York: Grove Press, 1959. Reprinted by permission of Grove/Atlantic, Inc. and Calder Publications Ltd.

Bellow, Saul. *Herzog*. Greenwich, CT: Fawcett, 1964.

Bettelheim, Bruno. *The Uses of Enchantment*. New York: Vintage (Random House), 1989.

Blackmur, R.P. *Form and Value in Modern Poetry*. Garden City, N.J: Doubleday, 1957.

Boas, George. Preface to *Myth, Religion and Mother Right*, by Johann Jakob Bachofen. London: Routledge and Kegan Paul, 1967.

Boorstin, Daniel. *The Discovers: A History of Man's Search to Know His World and Himself*. New York: Vintage (Random House), 1983.

Bradley, A.C. *Shakespearean Tragedy*. London: Macmillan, 1966.

Brown, Stephen J., S.J. *The World of Imagery*. New York: Haskell House, 1965.

Budden, Julian. *Verdi*. London: J.M. Dent, 1985; New York: Vintage, 1987.

Burgess, Anthony. *A Clockwork Orange*. New York: W.W. Norton, 1963. Published by William Heinemann. © Estate of Anthony Burgess. Reprinted by permission of The Random House Group Ltd and the Estate of Anthony Burgess.

Campbell, Joseph. *The Masks of God*. vol. 1: Primitive Mythology. New York: Penguin, 1976.

Catullus. *The Poems of Catullus*. Translated by Guy Lee. New York: Oxford University Press, 1991.

Caute, David. *The Great Fear: The Anti-Communist Purge Under Truman and Eisenhower*. New York: Simon and Schuster, 1978.

Chadwick, Henry. *The Early Church*. London: Penguin, 1993.

Chandler, Raymond. *The Big Sleep*. New York: Vintage (Random House), 1988. Copyright 1939 by Raymond Chandler and renewed 1967 by Helga Greene, Executrix of the Estate of Raymond Chandler. Used by permission of Alfred A. Knopf, a division of Random House, Inc.

Cicero, *Pro Archia Poeta Oratio*.

Collier, James Lincoln. *Benny Goodman and the Swing Era*. New York: Oxford University Press, 1989.

Conrad, Joseph. Preface to *A Personal Record*. London: Dent, 1946.

Dangerfield, George. *The Strange Death of Liberal England*. New York: Capricorn Books, 1961.

Darwin, Charles. *On the Origin of Species*. New York: Modern Library, 1998.

Davis, Earle. *The Flint and the Flame: The Artistry of Charles Dickens.* Columbia: University of Missouri Press, 1963.

Defoe, Daniel. *Robinson Crusoe.* New York: Penguin, 1965.

DeLillo, Don. *White Noise.* New York: Viking, 1985. Copyright © 1984, 1985 by Don DeLillo. Used by permission of Viking Penguin, a division of Penguin Putnam Inc.

Dickens, Charles. *A Tale of Two Cities.* London: Dent (Everyman's Library), 1906.

———. *Bleak House.* London: Dent (Everyman's Library), 1907.

———. *Dombey and Son.* London: Dent (Everyman's Library), 1907.

———. *Hard Times.* London, Thomas Nelson, 1901.

———. *The Pickwick Papers.* London: Collins, n.d.

Eco, Umberto. *The Name of the Rose.* New York: Warner, 1984.

Ellmann, Richard. *Yeats: The Man and the Masks.* New York: Macmillan, 1948; W. W. Norton, 1978.

Empson, William. *Seven Types of Ambiguity.* New York: Meridian (Noonday), 1955.

Faulkner, William. *Light in August.* New York: Random House, 1932.

———. "Pantaloon in Black." From *Go Down Moses.* New York: Modern Library, 1955.

Fiedler, Leslie. *Waiting for the End.* London: Jonathan Cape, 1965.

Fielding, Henry. *A Journey from this World to the Next.* London: Dent (Everyman's Library), 1973.

Forster, E.M. *Aspects of the Novel.* New York: Harcourt Brace, 1927, 1956.

———. *Where Angels Fear to Tread.* New York: Vintage (Random House), 1992.

Friedman, Norman. "Point of View in Fiction." In *Theory of the Novel.* Edited by Philip Stevick. New York: Free Press (Macmillan) 1967.

Frye, Northrop. *The Anatomy of Criticism.* Princeton, NJ: Princeton University Press, 1957. Copyright © 1957 by Princeton University Press. Reprinted by permission of Princeton University Press.

Gibbon, Edward. *The Decline and Fall of the Roman Empire.* New York: Modern Library, n.d.

Gilson, Etienne. *The Unity of Philosophical Experience.* New York: Scribner's 1937.

Gorgias. "Praise of Helen." Translated by LaRue Van Hook. *Classical World* (1923).

Graves, Robert, and Alan Hodge. *The Reader Over Your Shoulder.* New York: Vintage (Random House) 1979.

Hadas, Moses. *Hellenistic Culture.* New York: Norton, 1972.

Hammett, Dashiell. *The Glass Key.* New York: Alfred A. Knopf, 1931. Copyright 1931 by Alfred A. Knopf, Inc. and renewed 1959 by Dashiel Hammett. Used by permission of Alfred A. Knopf, a division of Random House, Inc.

Hartman, Geoffrey H. *Beyond Formalism: Literary Essays 1958-1970.* New Haven: Yale University Press, 1970.

Hawkes, John. "Agony of the Sailor," from *Second Skin.* New York: New Directions, 1964. Copyright © 1964 by John Hawkes. Reprinted by permission of New Directions Publishing Corp. and Janklow & Nesbit Associates, on behalf of the author.

Hemingway, Ernest. *A Farewell to Arms.* New York: Scribner's, 1969.

Highet, Gilbert. *Juvenal the Satirist.* Oxford: Clarendon Press, 1954.

———. *The Classical Tradition.* New York: Oxford University Press, 1957.

Hubbard, Margaret. *Propertius.* London: Duckworth, 1974. Reprinted by permission of the publisher.

Huizinga, J. *The Waning of the Middle Ages.* Translated by F. Hopman. Harmondsworth: Penguin (Peregrine), 1965.

Hume, David. *An Enquiry Concerning the Principles of Morals.* La Salle, IL: Open Court, 1966.

Hutchinson, Harold F. *The Hollow Crown.* New York: John Day Co., 1961.

James, Henry. *The Wings of the Dove*. New York: Signet (New American Library), 1964.

Johnson, Samuel. *Rasselas*. Oxford: Clarendon Press, 1898.

Joseph, Sister Miriam. *Rhetoric in Shakespeare's Time*. New York: Harcourt, Brace & World, 1962.

Joyce, James. *A Portrait of the Artist as a Young Man*. Harmondsworth: Penguin, 1960.

Kermode, Frank. *The Sense of an Ending*. New York: Oxford University Press, 1967.

Kesey, Ken. *One Flew Over the Cuckoo's Nest*. New York: Viking, 1962. Copyright © 1962, 1990 by Ken Kesey. Used by permission of Viking Penguin, a division of Penguin Putnam, Inc.

Knelman, Fred. *Nuclear Energy: The Unforgiving Technology*. Edmonton: Hurtig, 1976.

Knowles, David. *The Evolution of Medieval Thought*. New York: Vintage, 1962.

Krier, William J. "A Courtesy Which Grants Integrity: A Literal Reading of *Moll Flanders*," *ELH*, September 1971.

Laski, Marghanita. *Jane Austen and Her World*. Revised Edition. London: Thames and Hudson, 1975.

Lattimore, Richmond. *Story Patterns in Greek Tragedy*. Ann Arbor: University of Michigan Press, 1969.

Lawrence, D.H. *Women in Love*. Markham, ON: Penguin, 1960.

Lawrence, T.E. *Seven Pillars of Wisdom*. Harmondsworth: Penguin, 1962.

Lear, Linda. *Rachel Carson: Witness for Nature*. New York: Henry Holt, 1997.

Lloyd, A.L. *Folk Song in England*. London: Paladin (Granada), 1975.

Lowry, Malcolm. *Under the Volcano*. New York: Harper & Row, 1984.

Lyly, John. *Euphues: The Anatomy of Wit*. In *Elizabethan Fiction*. Edited by Robert Ashley and Edwin M. Mosley. New York: Holt, Rinehart and Winston, 1953.

McCourt, Frank. *Angela's Ashes*. London: HarperCollins, 1996. © Frank McCourt 1996. Reprinted by permission of HarperCollins Publishers Ltd. and Scribner, a Division of Simon & Schuster, Inc.

MacIntyre, Alasdair. *After Virtue*. Notre Dame, IN: University of Notre Dame Press, 1981. © 1981 University of Notre Dame Press.

Martin, Richard. "The Seven Sages as Performers of Wisdom." *Cultural Poetics in Archaic Greece*. Edited by Carol Dougherty and Leslie Kurke. New York: Oxford University Press, 1998.

Mayer, Leonard B. *Music, the Arts, and Ideas*. Chicago: University of Chicago Press, 1967.

Mead, Margaret. *New Lives for Old: Cultural Transformation—Manus, 1928–1953*. New York: Dell, 1956.

Michaels, Anne. *Fugitive Pieces*. Toronto: McClelland & Stewart, 1996. Used by permission, McClelland & Stewart Ltd. *The Canadian Publishers*.

Mill, J.S. *Auguste Comte and Positivism*. Ann Arbor: University of Michigan Press, 1961.

Miller, John C. *Alexander Hamilton and the Growth of the New Nation*. New York: Harper and Row, 1959.

Muir, Edwin. *The Structure of the Novel*. New York: Harbinger (Harcourt, Brace & World), n.d.

Nabokov, Vladimir. *Ada*. London: Weidenfeld and Nicolson, 1969.

Paton, Alan. *Cry, the Beloved Country*. New York: Scribner's, 1948.

Pavel, Thomas. *The Poetics of Plot*. Minneapolis: University of Minnesota Press, 1985.

Peradotto, John. *Man in the Middle Voice: Name and Narration in the Odyssey*. Princeton: Princeton University Press, 1990.

Quiller-Couch, Arthur. *On the Art of Writing*. New York: Capricorn 1961.

Read, Herbert. *English Prose Style*. New York: Henry Holt, 1928.

Rice, Anne. *Interview with the Vampire*. New York: Ballantine, 1977.

Richards, I.A. *The Philosophy of Rhetoric*. New York: Oxford University Press, 1965.

Richler, Mordecai. *The Street*. Markham, ON: Penguin, 1977.

Russell, Bertrand. "The Value of Free Thought." In *Understanding History*. New York: Philosophical Library, 1957.

Rubinstein, Arthur. *My Young Years*. New York: Alfred A. Knopf, 1973.

Rushdie, Salman. *Shame*. New York: Alfred A. Knopf, 1983.

Ryle, Gilbert. *Plato's Progress*. Cambridge: Cambridge University Press, 1966.

Saintsbury, George. *A History of English Prose Rhythm*. London: Macmillan, 1922.

Scheer, Robert. *With Enough Shovels*. New York: Random House, 1982.

Scholes, Robert, and Robert Kellogg. *The Nature of Narrative*. New York: Oxford University Press, 1966.

Schonberg, Harold C. *The Great Conductors*. New York: Simon and Schuster, 1967.

Shakespeare, William, *As You Like It*.

Shaw, George Bernard. *Man and Superman*. New York: Brentano's, 1905.

Snodgrass, Anthony. *Archaic Greece*. London: J.M. Dent, 1980; Berkeley: University of California Press, 1981.

Sontag, Susan. *Against Interpretation*. New York: Farrar, Straus & Giroux, 1966. Copyright © 1964, 1966, renewed 1994 by Susan Sontag. Reprinted by permission of Farrar, Straus and Giroux, LLC.

Stein, Gertrude. *Three Lives*. New York: Vintage (Random House), 1936.

Stevick, Philip. *The Chapter in Fiction*. Syracuse, NY: Syracuse University Press, 1970.

Stock, Noel. *The Life of Ezra Pound*. New York: Pantheon, 1970. Copyright © 1970 by Noel Stock. Used by permission of Pantheon Books, a division of Random House, Inc, and Routledge Ltd.

Sutherland, James. *On English Prose*. Toronto: University of Toronto Press, 1957.

Syme, Ronald. *Sallust*. Berkeley: University of California Press, 1964. Copyright © 1964, 1962 Regents of the University of California, renewed 1990 David Gill. Reprinted by permission of University of California Press.

Tawney, R.H. *Religion and the Rise of Capitalism*. New York: Penguin, 1947.

Taylor, A.J.P. *The Habsburg Monarchy: 1809–1918*. London: Penguin 1981.

Thomas, Francis-Noël, and Mark Turner. *Clear and Simple as the Truth*. Princeton: Princeton University Press, 1994.

Tillotson, Kathleen. "Dombey and Son." In *Dickens*. Edited by A.E. Dyson. New York: Aurora, 1970.

Trollope, Anthony. *The Warden*. Markham, ON: Penguin, 1984.

Urquhart, Jane. *The Underpainter*. Toronto: McClelland & Stewart, 1997. Used by permission, McClelland & Stewart Ltd. *The Canadian Publishers*.

White, E.B. *Stuart Little*. New York: Harper & Row, 1945, 1973; London: Hamish Hamilton, 1946. Copyright 1945 by E.B. White. Text copyright renewed © 1973 by E.B. White. Used by permission of HarperCollins Publishers.

Wiesel, Elie. *A Beggar in Jerusalem*. New York: Random House, 1970.

Williams, Joseph. *Style: Toward Clarity and Grace*. Chicago: University of Chicago Press, 1990.

Wilson, Edmund. *I Thought of Daisy*. New York: Farrar, Strauss & Giroux, 1967. Copyright © 1953 by Edmund Wilson. Reprinted by permission of Farrar, Straus and Giroux, LLC.

———. "Marxism and Literature." In *The Triple Thinkers and The Wound and the Bow*. Boston: Northeastern University Press, 1984. From *The Triple Thinkers: Twelve Essays on Literary Subjects* by Edmund Wilson. Copyright © 1948 by Edmund Wilson. Copyright renewed 1975 by Elena Wilson. Reprinted by permission of Farrar, Straus and Giroux, LLC.

Wilson, Edward O. *The Diversity of Life*. New York: Norton, 1999.

Wimsatt, William. *The Prose Style of Samuel Johnson*. New Haven: Yale University Press, 1963.

Yeazell, Ruth Bernard. *Language and Knowledge in the Late Novels of Henry James.* Chicago: University of Chicago Press, 1976.

Zierer, Otto. *History of Germany.* Translated by G. Irvins. New York: Leon Amiel, 1977.

INDEX